The Russian Economy: A Very Short Introduction

T0055134

VERY SHORT INTRODUCTIONS are for anyone wanting a stimulating and accessible way into a new subject. They are written by experts, and have been translated into more than 45 different languages.

The series began in 1995, and now covers a wide variety of topics in every discipline. The VSI library currently contains over 650 volumes—a Very Short Introduction to everything from Psychology and Philosophy of Science to American History and Relativity—and continues to grow in every subject area.

Very Short Introductions available now:

Available soon:

For more information visit our website

www.oup.com/vsi/

Richard Connolly

THE RUSSIAN ECONOMY

A Very Short Introduction

OXFORD
UNIVERSITY PRESS

Great Clarendon Street, Oxford, OX2 6DP,
United Kingdom

Oxford University Press is a department of the University of Oxford.
It furthers the University's objective of excellence in research, scholarship,
and education by publishing worldwide. Oxford is a registered trade mark of
Oxford University Press in the UK and in certain other countries

First edition published in 2020

Impression: 1

Published in the United States of America by Oxford University Press
198 Madison Avenue, New York, NY 10016, United States of America

British Library Cataloguing in Publication Data

Data available

Library of Congress Control Number: 2020936004

ISBN 978-0-19-884890-5

Printed in Great Britain by
Ashford Colour Press Ltd, Gosport, Hampshire

Contents

List of illustrations

Chapter 1
Forces that shaped the economy in Russia

On the eve of the millennium, Russia's prime minister, and soon-to-be president, Vladimir Putin, surveyed the state of the Russian economy. After the collapse of the Soviet Union at the end of 1991, the Russian Federation emerged as a new state in the international order. Its leaders attempted to build a new type of political and economic system—a market democracy—that, it was hoped, would see Russia become a 'normal' Western country with democratic freedoms, a market economy, a well-functioning state, and high incomes. However, when Putin looked back on what had been a turbulent decade—even by Russian standards—he showed in a frank and honest fashion just how far Russia had failed to realize these lofty aspirations.

In what became known as his 'millennium manifesto', Putin lamented that Russia had slipped behind the world's major powers. The overall size of the Russian economy was much smaller than it had been only a decade before. The average Russian citizen's income was among the lowest in Europe. A decade of rapid growth was needed if income levels were to reach those of Spain and Portugal, themselves far from the richest of the European powers. Russia had also slipped down the rankings on measures of innovation and technological development. For a country that only a few years before had led the world in areas like space exploration and nuclear physics, this represented a sharp reversal of fortunes. Lawlessness and weak property rights discouraged Russia's citizens from investing in new commercial ventures. As a result, investment by Russians and foreigners was much lower than was needed to generate economic growth and an improvement in living standards.

Putin's lugubrious assessment of the state that Russia found itself in at the beginning of the millennium was brutal in its honesty. But in doing so, Putin became the latest in a long series of Russian (and Soviet) leaders who had displayed a sharp awareness of the country's economic deficiencies. Weaknesses in Russia's legal system, underinvestment in modern economic activities, technological underdevelopment, and lower living standards than other major powers were all characteristics of the Russian economy that had endured over centuries. Putin, it seemed, was grappling with much the same problems that his Soviet and tsarist predecessors had found before him. To understand why certain characteristics of the Russian economy have proven so hard to change, we need to go back 500 years, to the period when modern Russia was formed.

The Russian empire emerged in the mid-1500s when Eurasia was in a state of extreme flux. The horse-borne nomadic groups that had dominated the Eurasian steppe since the expansion of the Golden Horde in the 12th and 13th centuries began to weaken and then disintegrate, and they were gradually displaced by a number of large, more centralized empires. These included the Ottoman and Safavid empires to the south, and the Qing empire to the east. In the north-west of the Eurasian land mass, the Russian empire materialized from the Grand Principality of Moscow, or Muscovy for short, under the leadership of Ivan IV, or 'the Terrible' (1530–84).

The Russian empire that subsequently took shape was influenced both by its past, when it was ruled by the descendants of Genghis Khan and the Golden Horde, and by the challenges its rulers faced as they attempted to build a viable state amidst external conflict and the struggle for domestic consolidation of imperial power. Any appreciation of why the Russian economy developed in the way that it did over the past 500 years requires at least a basic understanding of how these early efforts at state-building exerted a strong influence over the country's subsequent economic development. Over time, several core characteristics crystallized to form what can be described as the Russian national system of political economy. According to the scholar of international political economy Robert Gilpin, each national system of political economy differs in many important respects, but three are of particular importance: (1) the primary purposes of economic activity within a country; (2) the role of the state in the economy; and (3) the structure of private business.

Gilpin argues that societies vary in the extent to which they emphasize broad objectives, which might include consumer welfare or the pursuit of national power. This in turn often shapes the role played by the state in the economy. Economies like the UK and the USA, for example, that tend to emphasize consumer welfare see a correspondingly weaker role played by the state in the economy, while those that emphasize national power tend to be characterized by greater state influence. The role of the state in an economy in turn shapes the nature and structure of business in an economy. America's relatively dispersed business structure, for instance, reflects the generally non-interventionist nature of the state. By contrast, countries where the state is the dominant actor in the economy tend to permit only weak private sectors. Examining Russia's economic history along these three dimensions reveals a very specific type of economy.

The purpose of economic activity in Russia

Throughout the past 500 years, Russia's history has been characterized by episodes of immense violence, caused by both external conflict and internal instability. As Muscovy became the

Russian empire in the 16th century, Russia's rulers were engaged in fierce competition with several strong powers to the north and west, such as the Swedish and Polish-Lithuanian empires, and, in the south and east, with an altogether different threat in the form of nomadic raiders such as the Tatar, Nogai, and Kalmyk bands. The states in the north and west were similar to other powerful European states of that time, possessing sophisticated systems of state control, taxation, and well-organized military forces. The nomadic bands roaming in the south and east were not as well organized, but they were no less dangerous. As well as regularly destroying property and forcibly taking local people into slavery on Russia's frontiers, raiders also represented a serious military threat. In 1571, for example, Crimean Tatars were able to sack Moscow itself.

Lacking any real clear or natural geographically defined borders, such as those imposed by coastlines, large lakes and rivers, or mountain ranges, Russia contested its borders with all its neighbours. To be sure, most other states and empires in Europe and Eurasia faced similar problems. But the scale of the challenge facing Russia was greater, largely because it faced a wider range of different threats, from the modern, well-equipped armies concentrated in the north and west to the dispersed but more numerous raiders penetrating Russia's enormous and porous frontier to its south and east. This, according to the historian Geoffrey Hosking, meant 'its army had to be flexible [and] disproportionately large for the size of its population'.

The demands imposed by having to deal with these multiple threats to its sovereignty meant that a large part of the Russian empire's formative years was spent subordinating all other concerns to those of security. The coordination of large fighting forces across one of the largest geographically contiguous empires in the world demanded a high degree of central control. This resulted in very specific forms of state organization that enabled its rulers to mobilize the resources needed to fight and win wars.

These forms of organizational and institutional development ultimately proved effective, at least in military terms, and by passing the ultimate test of state survival, Russia was able to first resist and then later defeat and dominate the Polish-Lithuanian empire. Later, in the 18th and 19th centuries, Russia was militarily capable enough to compete at different times with Britain, France, and other European powers. Most spectacularly, Russia's armies played the decisive role in defeating Napoleon's Grande Armée in the early 19th century.

To the south and east, Russian forces gradually but inexorably secured and then dominated the great Eurasian steppe frontier that separated it from the Ottoman, Persian, and Chinese empires. In doing so, Russia's territory in the south and east grew at a much faster rate than it did in the west. This expansion was both the cause of external conflict and a consequence. But a direct outcome of this brisk expansion was the creation of a territorially large and contiguous, but multi-ethnic, empire. This was in stark contrast to a typical European empire, the territories of which were usually spread across the world, far from its European metropole. Consequently, Russia's territorial expansion led to the deliberate aggrandizement and transformation of numerous and disparate new territories and populations. According to Hosking, this meant that Russia was an empire but not a cohesive nation of the type that emerged across western Europe at around the same time. This increased the scope for internal instability, with Russian history punctuated by episodes of extreme disorder as the central state periodically failed to keep a lid on the empire's heterogeneous and often volatile subjects.

The paramount importance of maintaining internal order and external security—often two sides of the same coin—caused security concerns to dominate economic development in a way that few other countries have ever experienced. While all countries must ensure external and internal security as a first order objective of statehood, for Russia these concerns were a permanent and enduring aspect of the country's existence. As a result, there have been very few moments in Russian history where economic activity has not been subordinated to security concerns, with Russia spending a higher proportion of its national income on defence and security than most other major global powers. Mobilizing the resources required to maintain adequate armed forces to deal with the array of potential threats facing Russia, while simultaneously ensuring domestic cohesion and order, has meant that economic policy and the allocation of resources were often carried out in a highly centralized fashion. This resulted in an excessively strong state and a chronically weak private sector.

The role of the state

The state has been the dominant force throughout Russia's history, whether in the form of the imperial state of the tsars or later in the guise of the bureaucrats who took their orders from the communist party. The Russian economist and former policymaker Yegor Gaidar traced the roots of this dominance to the decision of the Muscovite grand princes to maintain the onerous Mongol taxation system even after the successors to the Golden Horde were overthrown in the 15th and 16th centuries. Instead of allowing local princes to reduce their tribute to their rulers, the central authorities in Moscow simply replaced the Horde as the beneficiary of the punitive system of taxation. This maximized the financial resources available to the state, and enabled Moscow to maintain large and effective armed forces that were able to guarantee the empire's independence. And it also helped secure the loyalty of the rulers of local populations in those areas into which the Russian empire expanded, as Russia's leaders granted local elites opportunities for personal enrichment. But it came at the expense of the wider population, and suppressed the emergence of a healthy and vibrant class of independent property owners.

One especially important way in which the Russian imperial state was able to generate both military capabilities and tax revenues was through the *pomeshchiki* (service estate-holders). These *pomeshchiki* were essentially landowners who held their property and privileges (*pomestie*) in return for providing military service to the state. As the empire grew and developed, these service estate-holders paid money to the central treasury and exacted services from the population residing on their land. Known as *kormlenie* (feeding), this raised the incentive for both the state and the landowners to ensure that control over the population was tight. After all, this facilitated greater revenues for the landowners and, in turn, for the state, resulting in the emergence of a sophisticated network of patron–client relations in which revenue generation was devolved to agents working on behalf of the state. Initially, landowners and boyars carried out these duties; later, state bureaucrats performed similar functions. For Gaidar, the essence of this system in which the welfare of the general population was suppressed to serve the interests of the state only came to an end with the collapse of the Soviet Union in 1991.

One of the most important consequences of this network of patron–client relations was that obligations to patrons were more important than obligations under the law. For as long as Russia's rulers received the taxes they needed to pursue their wider state objectives, they rarely concerned themselves with how the agents of the state extracted this income. As the economists Steven Rosefielde and Stefan Hedlund put it: 'It was a callous mechanism for squeezing taxes from a servile population, but...Russia's autocrats didn't systematically oppress the people or bother themselves about their plight. They simply permitted their servitors to get the job done whatever that entailed.' This meant that throughout Russia's imperial history (and arguably long after), the core mechanism of governance was not rule of law, but instead the rule of men, in which the patrimonial granting of access to revenues and resources underpinned state control.

The use of servitors to extract revenue and help govern the empire's vast territories also explains a long-running paradox in Russia's political and economic history: a state with very few formal controls over the behaviour of its leaders and officials often only exercised weak control over its population in practice. In times of crisis the Russian state was often able to mobilize huge financial and material resources in pursuit of state objectives, whether they were the defeat of foreign powers during times of external conflict or in the implementation of grand state projects, such as the construction of St Petersburg under Peter the Great in the late 1600s and early 1700s. But, on a more mundane day-to-day level, when the attentions of Russia's supreme rulers have been elsewhere, the delegated agents of the state—whether they be landowners, regional bosses, or individual bureaucrats—were granted so much autonomy to achieve their assigned objectives that they ruled their areas as if they were their own personal fiefdoms.

In practical terms, the dominance of the patrimonial state in Russia resulted in it playing a pronounced role in 'strategic' industries, especially those related to military-industrial production, while neglecting non-strategic activities. As a result, many industries that would prove to be of importance in underpinning state power at different points in history— metallurgy, railways, and heavy industry—were often placed under some form of state control. Very often, these enterprises were relatively inefficient and incapable of surviving without state support and protection. Because of their links with the state, they were not subjected to market discipline and were able to survive despite their weaknesses. Indeed, the state often intervened in markets to ensure that the playing field benefited those owners and firms that worked with the state. Independent property owners of the type that emerged in Britain during the industrial revolution, for example, were not tolerated.

The dominance of the state distorted and often repressed the generally decentralized allocation of resources that takes place in market economies, that is, through the independent decisions made by households and firms. As a result, a number of structural deficiencies in the economy persisted throughout Russia's history, including: a weak financial system that tends to allocate capital only to firms linked with the state; a poor legal environment that acts as a disincentive to entrepreneurial activity; and a low level of competition caused by the dominance of large, state-owned or state-linked firms in the economy that suppress innovation. State campaigns to mobilize resources in the economy were usually based on coercion rather than the initiative of market-based organizations. The market's weakness also meant that any period of 'catch-up' with neighbouring powers was undertaken only under the initiative of the state. With the private sector weak, and the state sometimes unable or unwilling actively to promote economic development, Russia has often been dependent on taxing its most abundant resources: labour and natural resources.

Private business in Russia

A logical corollary of this tendency towards state intervention in the economy was that private property rights in Russia were always weak. To be sure, private property and independent business always existed on a significant scale in Russia, at least until the construction of the centrally planned economy in the late 1920s. But property rights were always poorly protected and conditional on good relations with the state. This usually required property owners to both share a sizeable slice of commercially generated revenues with the state, and to provide resources quickly to the state in times of emergency. If these conditions were not met, or if property owners demonstrated too much independence from the state, private property might be seized and reallocated to individuals who were more inclined to support the state's activities.

As a result, the nature of private business in Russia has always been overshadowed by the threat of expropriation. In practice, this meant that owners who had sufficiently strong ties with influential state officials tended to enjoy stronger property rights than those who did not. As such, property rights in Russia were not homogeneous; instead, their strength in each case depended on other factors beyond legal title, not least the strength of an owner's political connections. This has always been a serious problem for economic development in Russia because poorly protected property rights increased uncertainty for a large proportion of would-be and actual entrepreneurs. The incentive to invest in new productive capabilities such as factories, new technologies, or in acquiring well-qualified workers was drastically reduced. After all, why do all these things if you were unsure that you would own your property long enough to enjoy the fruits of your labour? And why bother introducing costly innovations if you were confident that state officials would restrict your ability to market and sell your goods and services?

A far more reliable way to make money was to connive with state officials and block the emergence of competitors, which further reduced innovation and investment in new technologies. This led to Russia appearing as a giant with clay feet among its Western competitors. As the Enlightenment was followed by the Industrial Revolution across large swathes of north-western Europe and its colonial offshoots, Russia's model of political economy produced comparatively unsatisfactory results. It was, to be sure, a large economy. Its large population and abundant natural resources made sure of this. But in per capita terms, it was among the poorest of the so-called 'great powers' dominating the international arena. As other countries built new industries, located in rapidly growing cities, Russia remained a laggard in technological terms, with most of its population continuing to reside in the countryside. This prevented the sort of rapid growth in incomes and living standards observed in the world's leading powers during this period. It also blunted Russia's military prowess.

These weaknesses were brutally exposed in the Crimean War (1853–6), prompting Russia's rulers to engage in a long, painful, and only partially successful process of social and economic reform. The country made rapid, if somewhat uneven, progress in catching up with its peer competitors by industrializing and urbanizing at the end of the 19th and the beginning of the 20th centuries. However, just as it seemed to be on the verge of catching up with its more modern competitors, the imperial Russian state failed in the ultimate test of war, first with Japan (1904–5) and then with Germany and the Austro-Hungarian empire in the First World War. Defeat in 1918 was followed by revolution and civil war, resulting in the overthrow of the imperial social order. Nevertheless, the three core elements of the Russian system of political economy—an excessive focus on security, a dominant state, and a weak market—would endure long after the demise of the imperial order.

Chapter 2
The Soviet planned economy

After the Russian revolution and subsequent civil war, the newly created Soviet Union was ruled by a sole victorious party, the Bolsheviks, who renamed themselves the Communist Party of the Soviet Union (CPSU). As the country began to recover from the ravages of nearly a decade of warfare, a historically new type of economy was created: the centrally planned economy. According to the economist Vladimir Kontorovich, the construction of such an economic system, in which an entire economic order was uprooted and replaced with one based on diametrically opposite principles, was 'the greatest economic experiment in history'.

During the civil war, the Bolsheviks ran the economy in those areas under their control with an iron fist. Entire industries were placed under the control of the authorities, market freedoms curtailed, and strict controls over trade and enterprise were put in place. This draconian system, known as 'war communism' (or *voyennyy kommunizm*), in which the state mobilized scarce resources by crushing living standards, helped the Bolsheviks prevail in the military conflict. It also left the population exhausted. With the war over, people quickly began to demand an end to the excessive discipline and privations demanded by war communism.

The country's new leader, Vladimir Lenin (1870–1924), relaxed state control over the economy in 1921 in an effort both to boost economic growth and to generate support for the new communist order. War communism was replaced by the New Economic Policy (NEP), which, according to Lenin, would be a system that included the 'free market and capitalism, but both subject to state control'. NEP partially reversed the complete nationalization of industry of war communism and permitted small-scale private enterprise. It was especially popular in the countryside where most Russians continued to live and work. State control remained in place in the strategically important 'commanding heights' of the economy, including heavy industry and banking.

NEP was initially seen as a temporary expedient designed to relax the pressure on the population and generate support for the new communist leadership. However, for many in the CPSU, it was a concession too far. These revolutionaries believed that a truly communist society needed to be built with greater urgency. They believed that the class enemy—capitalists that remained in the country—needed to be defeated before it staged a counter-revolution, that the country needed to industrialize quickly to be strong enough to defeat external capitalist states, and that the Soviet Union should join with workers—the proletariat—from other industrialized countries to foment revolution and spark a global communist revolution.

Lenin was left incapacitated and unable to rule after suffering a series of illnesses from 1921 onwards, and a period of collective leadership followed his death in 1924. The fate of NEP and the future of the country's direction of economic development became a key dividing line among those who wished to lead the Soviet Union. Those who believed in the continuation of a mixed economy along the lines of NEP were defeated by those, eventually led by Joseph Stalin (1878–1953), who advocated the rapid state-led industrialization of the country in a fashion that resembled the war communism that had only recently been abandoned.

Stalin emerged as the country's leader by 1928. While NEP succeeded in returning industrial and agricultural production to pre-war (1913) levels, he felt that it was necessary to transform the Soviet Union from what was still largely an agrarian economy to a modern industrial, socialist economy. To do this, he oversaw a period of rapid industrialization based on a series of legally binding five-year plans devised and executed by the communist state authorities. These plans required a 'big push' in rates of investment in heavy industry at the expense of consumption and the living standards of the general population, especially those residing in the countryside.

To promote industrialization—which, in the 1920s and 1930s, meant coal and steel production, electrification, and the construction of automobiles—vast new enterprises were constructed at breakneck speed. These included the enormous steel-production facility at Magnitogorsk in the Ural Mountains, the largest of its kind in the world at the time. Industrialization, and economic policy more broadly, was overseen by Gosplan, or the State Planning Committee, which coordinated industrial activity on behalf of the CPSU. Gosplan issued commands to different ministries and enterprises, and monitored their implementation. Amidst the chaos of rapid urbanization and industrialization, the illusion of Gosplan control over the economy was often greater than the reality. Nevertheless, its power and influence was vastly higher from the 1920s onwards than it was under NEP.

The leadership of the CPSU, and through it, the technocrats in Gosplan, were more concerned with increasing the volume of industrial production than they were with whether these enterprises generated a profit. Much of the increase in production took place in industries that served to bolster Soviet military power. State funds were used to ensure that enterprises could not 'go bust'. Known as soft budget constraints, the removal of the need to generate profits meant that enterprise directors were incentivized to invest and expand production, resulting in rapid industrial and economic growth. Although the data for the period are unreliable and open to different interpretations, it is clear that most branches of heavy industry grew by anywhere between 350 and 600 per cent between 1928 and 1938. Growth was especially brisk in industries needed to support the expansion of military capabilities. Defence-industrial production of tanks, aircraft, and submarines grew at an even faster rate of 1,200–1,800 per cent. Production of consumer goods, by contrast, grew much more slowly, although living standards did begin to rise in the 1930s for those who lived in urban areas. Overall, the economy grew, even by the most conservative estimates, at around 6 per cent annually between 1928 and 1940. This growth took place against the background of the Great Depression, which caused many in the advanced capitalist countries to question whether the market was as effective as state direction in ensuring economic growth.

The roots of the Soviet economy's emphasis on heavy industry were partly found in the veneration of industry that was a feature of Marxist thought. But it was also caused by a desire to create military power, which in turn was a consequence of the chronic sense of isolation felt by the Soviet leadership. Until the end of the Chinese Civil War in 1949, the USSR was the only major socialist power in the world. As a result, its leaders felt a deep sense of insecurity and fear of foreign invasion, first from 'Western imperialists' and then from Fascist Germany. Understandably, the Soviet leadership saw a strong industrial base as a vital necessity for a strong, self-sufficient Soviet military. This, according to Stalin, needed to be done quickly. 'We are lagging behind them by 50–100 years,' he argued; 'unless we close that gap in 10 years, we'll be crushed.'

The price of industrialization was largely paid by those living in the countryside. During the first five-year plan, the Soviet leadership decided to integrate individual farms and labour into collectively controlled (*kholkozy*) and state-controlled farms (*sovkhozy*). In theory, this move was to be undertaken voluntarily. In practice, the Soviet leadership forced the majority of peasants to move onto collective farms. Severe controls were put in place to limit the ability of peasants to travel outside their villages or to change their place of work. In areas where the peasantry resisted, the state resorted to waging what amounted to civil war against them, using armed force and mass violence to enforce its will.

In the eyes of the Soviet leadership, collectivization had a number of advantages. It was ideologically preferable as it put an end to large-scale ownership of private property. Stalin regarded the more industrious and well-earning peasants, labelled *kulaks* (or 'fists'), as class enemies and a potential source of counter-revolution. Bringing the peasantry under state supervision in collective farms also made it easier for the authorities to plan economic activity as they did in the towns and cities. Perhaps most importantly, the state was able to pay significantly lower prices for agricultural output. Much of this output, especially grain, was sold on international markets to finance imports of machinery needed for industrialization. By 1937, collectivization was to all intents and purposes complete. Over 90 per cent of the Soviet peasantry were residing and working on collective farms.

In quantitative terms this was a remarkable achievement. However, the human cost of collectivization was catastrophic. Millions of peasants—rich *kulak*s or otherwise—had their property taken from them, and were deported from their home villages, arrested, or shot. Collectivization caused disastrous famines across the main food-producing areas of the Soviet Union, including Ukraine, central and southern Russia, and Kazakhstan. Estimates of the death toll vary, but mid-range assessments indicate that around 6–8 million people died as a result of collectivization. The majority of those who died were from Ukraine, resulting in what Ukrainians call the *Holodomor* ('death by hunger'). Many more peasants were sent to the GULAG—the state labour camps—where forced labour was used in the construction of important infrastructure across the country. With the incentive for collective farmworkers to work much reduced, agricultural yields and productivity declined. While agricultural output later recovered, the agrarian sector of the Soviet economy would remain the Achilles heel of the economy until the Soviet Union disintegrated in 1991. Not for the first time in Russian history, the general population was forced to bear the burden of the political leadership pursuing objectives related to state security.

By the mid-1930s, the core features of what became known as the Stalinist planned economy were in place. They included: the overarching role played by Marxist-Leninist ideology in justifying both the political monopoly of the CPSU and state ownership of the means of production (i.e. all factories and industrial enterprises); the bureaucratic allocation of resources, with the broad objectives formulated by the CPSU leadership and managed by Gosplan; the use of elaborate multi-year plans as the basis for the allocation and management of resources to and in different sectors and enterprises of the economy; the system of fixed prices where prices were not the result of supply and demand, but instead based on calculations made by bureaucrats; the bureaucratic control of employment and wages; and state management of foreign trade.

In many ways, the centrally planned economy represented an extreme version of the more traditional Russian system of political economy. The state, which was always dominant in the imperial Russian economy as noted in Chapter 1, was, after the end of the 1920s, the sole force in the Soviet economy. State ownership of the means of production was an essential part of this system as the elimination of private property gave the state monopoly power within the economy. This was a precondition for, and complementary to, the CPSU's monopoly on political power. It was also an essential element of official ideology. The only private property that remained after the late 1920s was confined to people's personal effects and small allotments used to grow relatively small quantities of food for personal consumption.

An important consequence of state ownership of the means of production was that all major decisions over the allocation of resources—prices, investment, consumption, and trade with the wider global economy—were ultimately made by a small number of the ruling CPSU's most senior leaders. Objectives were formulated by the upper echelons of the party, the Politburo and the Central Committee, and the necessary actions to fulfil these goals were transmitted down to party functionaries. Enforcing the will of the leadership and ensuring that the economy served the requirements of the party meant that economic activity was conducted on strictly hierarchical lines. Legally binding orders were given from above, and those lower down in the hierarchy were tasked with implementing those commands.

The economic system that was built in the 1930s, and then rebuilt after the destruction caused by the Second World War (or what the Russians refer to as the Great Patriotic War), was characterized by excessive production in sectors that were deemed to be of political importance to the party leadership. In practice, this meant that a large proportion of the country's resources was allocated towards investment in heavy industry (later including oil and gas, and the nuclear power industry), on the one hand, and the huge military-industrial complex, on the other. Only a relatively small proportion of national income was made available for consumption.

This emphasis on investment in heavy industry and defence meant that while many Soviet workers had jobs in factories, the production of many consumer goods, including certain types of food, was relatively low. However, the prices of goods sold in shops were set at an artificially low level by the state authorities in the State Committee for Prices (*Goskomtsen*). As officials acting on behalf of a state that claimed to rule on behalf of the working class, they were obliged to set the price of staple goods—such as bread, milk, and butter—at affordable levels. The problem was that the combination of low prices and limited production caused chronic and widespread shortages for a wide range of different consumer products. Soviet consumers could afford these goods, but more often than not, these goods were not widely available on shop shelves. As a result, Soviet consumers were always worse served than their counterparts in capitalist economies. Ownership of consumer goods, such as cars, refrigerators, and telephones, that was taken for granted in the West from the 1960s onwards, was much lower in the Soviet Union. People often had to wait for years to buy even low-quality goods. This was not a problem for senior state officials who had access to special closed shops in which a wider range of higher-quality goods was available. This led to the Hungarian economist Janos Kornai describing Soviet-type systems as shortage economies. These shortages were a feature of Soviet life until the system disintegrated in 1991.

Once the planned economy was built towards the end of the 1920s, the communist leadership exercised much greater control over the country's interaction with the global economy. The revolutionaries who took control of Russia in 1917 initially hoped that communist rule would be the first step in the collapse of capitalism across the world and that socialism would extend across Europe and the wider world. However, as revolutionary movements elsewhere failed to topple any more of the major capitalist powers, and after Joseph Stalin emerged ascendant within the USSR, the outward-looking internationalism of the socialist movement soon gave way to a more introverted 'socialism in one country'.

Relations between the USSR and the rest of the capitalist world remained tense after the consolidation of Soviet power. This meant that the period of breakneck industrialization that took place from the late 1920s onwards was largely conducted away from the outside world. To be sure, the Soviet Union was not entirely isolated. It was, for example, one of the world's largest exporters of oil and grain in the 1930s, and these export revenues were used to finance the acquisition of foreign machinery and machine tools vital to industrialization. However, international trade was almost entirely planned and controlled by Gosplan. State-owned firms could not, for example, make contact with a foreign firm to conduct commercial relations without the express permission of the state authorities.

For Soviet planners, trade was conceived in very narrow terms: goods were exported to generate hard currency, which would in turn finance imports of technology or some consumer goods that could not be produced domestically. Moreover, central planning and control eliminated the effects of the price mechanism and international competition. International prices did not correspond with domestic Soviet prices for most goods, while the bureaucratic allocation of imports insulated Soviet enterprises from international competition. This meant that the traditional mechanisms through which international trade affects a domestic economy—price and competition—were absent from the Soviet Union. Bizarre outcomes ensued, such as imported high-technology machinery being assigned the same price in domestic rouble terms as much inferior Soviet analogues.

The Soviet economy after the Great Patriotic War

This rapidly industrialized system built under Stalin's rule provided the resources with which the Soviet Union was able to defeat Nazi Germany in the Second World War and emerge as one of only two superpowers. For large parts of the war, Soviet industry was able to outproduce Nazi Germany in a wide range of key items of military production. This enabled the Red Army to eventually overwhelm the vast bulk of Germany's armed forces deployed on the Eastern Front, albeit at great material and human cost.

The victory of the Soviet Union in the Second World War, and the subsequent Soviet-backed communist seizure of power across most of central and eastern Europe, presented the USSR with the opportunity to establish trading relations with a new group of ideologically friendly countries. The formation of the Council for Mutual Economic Assistance (CMEA) in 1949, ostensibly in response to the introduction of the Marshall Plan in Western Europe, generated much closer ties within the new socialist bloc. To many in the West—and, indeed, to many in the socialist countries of central and eastern Europe—this represented a Soviet empire.

Initially it was hoped that most external trade for CMEA members would take place within the bloc. As the economies of the region recovered from the destruction of the war this is precisely what happened: intra-bloc trade accelerated, and countries like East Germany, Czechoslovakia, and Romania served as reliable sources of relatively advanced machinery for the Soviet Union. However, after the 1950s the countries of the bloc began to trade increasingly with non-CMEA states. It was clear that while bloc autarky was ideologically desirable, in practice it failed to provide its members with the goods that they needed.

Even as the Soviet empire grew after 1945, security concerns continued to distort the economy. After paying a huge human price, both in building the Soviet planned economy in the 1930s and 1940s, and then in defeating Nazi Germany in the war, a new threat emerged in the form of the Cold War ideological struggle with the United States and its allies. The Cold War heightened the sense of insecurity felt by Stalin and other senior Soviet leaders. As a result, the leadership sanctioned the allocation of vast resources to the construction of even greater quantities of weapons, including the development of nuclear weapons and missile delivery systems. Giant arms factories were built, many of which were located deep in the Soviet Union, well away from where any putative invasion from the West would reach. This all

The Soviet planned economy

took place even as many Soviet citizens struggled to find housing and relied on rationed food.

Despite the onset of the Cold War, the consumption needs of the population were finally given greater attention after Stalin's death in 1953. Soviet citizens had endured great hardships before, during, and after the war. Housing was a particular problem and consumer goods remained scarce. Nikita Khrushchev (1894–1971) emerged as the successor to Stalin, and he recognized the need to make life more comfortable for the long-suffering population. As a result, investment in the production of consumer goods and housing rose. Changes in the incentive structure for workers in the agricultural sector were also made in the hope that they would increase food production.

Under Khrushchev, a sense of optimism began to pervade Soviet life. Many believed that a more humane version of socialism could emerge and potentially supersede its richer capitalist ideological opponents. In 1961, Khrushchev confidently predicted that the Soviet Union would reach the utopian stage of development known as communism by 1980. Indeed, post-war reconstruction generated a brisk rate of economic growth. In the 1950s, the income gap between the Soviet Union and its capitalist adversaries began to narrow. Soviet scientific achievements, including advances made in nuclear power, space exploration, and the construction of long-range ballistic missiles, convinced many that the Soviet model, once devoid of its worst Stalinist excesses, might represent a superior form of social order.

However, even as Khrushchev spoke of 'overtaking and surpassing the United States', the general level of productivity within the economy began to wilt as the growth in supply of inputs, such as labour, land, and capital, began to decline (Table 1). Consequently, economic growth began to wane steadily towards the end of the 1960s. This decline was manifested in a slower rate of technological innovation than Western countries (at least in non-military

Table 1. Soviet growth in inputs, output, and productivity, 1928–85 (annual average percentage change)

	1928–40	1950–60	1960–70	1970–5	1975–80	1980–5
Gross National Product (GNP)	5.8	5.7	5.2	3.7	2.6	2
Labour	3.3	1.2	1.7	1.7	1.2	0.7
Capital	9	9.5	8	7.9	6.8	6.3
Land	1.6	3.3	0.2	1	-0.1	-0.1
Productivity	1.7	1.6	1.5	0	-0.4	-0.5

Note: Data for 1940s omitted due to impact of the Second World War.

Source: Adapted from Gur Ofer, 'Soviet Economic Growth: 1928–1985', *Journal of Economic Literature*, 25/4 (Dec. 1987), 1767–1833, at 1778–9.

products) and in the continued failure of the Soviet economy to satisfy the needs of consumers. Despite some improvements under Khrushchev, foodstuffs and other consumer products were, in general, either of poor quality or of limited availability.

Stagnation and the emergence of the Soviet Union as a 'petro power'

Khrushchev's attempts to build a more humane form of socialism resulted in internal opposition. His attempts to increase efficiency by weakening the power of vast industrial ministries that emerged under Stalin created powerful opponents who eventually conspired to remove him from power in 1964. A new collective leadership took control, led by Leonid Brezhnev (1906–82), Alexei Kosygin, and Nikolai Podgorny, although over time this was dominated by Brezhnev. Under Brezhnev, the Soviet leadership grappled with how to reinvigorate the economy. A series of policy changes—known as the Kosygin reforms after the prime minister and architect of the reforms—was made to great fanfare in 1965. While these plans were designed to improve the incentives for Soviet enterprise directors and workers to increase efficiency, the key tenets of the Stalinist system remained unchanged.

The system of planning, which proved effective at stimulating extensive growth—that is, growth based on increasing the rate of investment in fixed capital and in moving people from low-productivity jobs in the countryside to higher-productivity jobs in urban factories—was ill suited to generating intensive growth based on squeezing out more output from the same number of inputs. Unsurprisingly, productivity rates continued the decline that began under Khrushchev. By the early 1970s, Kosygin's reforms had essentially been abandoned.

Instead of fundamentally reforming the system, efforts were made to make the existing system work better. To this end, planners embarked on ambitious but costly efforts to develop the Soviet

Union's vast and resource-rich hinterland in the Arctic and Siberia. This resulted in millions of people moving to cold and remote areas of the Soviet Union to expand production in the extraction of natural resources such as gold, diamonds, oil, and gas. This was hugely expensive as it involved building vastly expensive new infrastructure in forbidding climatic conditions. Higher wages, subsidized energy, and access to scarce goods were also used to induce millions of people to move to outposts in the Arctic and Siberia. However, the true cost was disguised by the Soviet Union's system of state-administered prices, which enabled the leaders to conceal the real price of populating some of the most remote and inhospitable areas on earth.

The discovery and subsequent exploitation of huge oil deposits in western Siberia during the 1960s led to a huge increase in oil production from 1970 onwards. Coinciding with the first oil shock in 1973, caused by the Yom Kippur War in the Middle East, it stimulated even greater Soviet investment in oil and gas production. As Soviet oil production grew, more oil was sold to Russia's capitalist rivals. Oil exports to OECD (Organization for Economic Cooperation and Development) countries grew from just over $2 billion in 1972 to over $25 billion by 1980. Accompanied by rising gas exports to western Europe, as well as the periodic sale of gold reserves, the Soviet Union was easily able to fund its considerable and growing import bill even as domestic productivity continued to decline.

As well as providing hard currency for imports of food and machinery, the absence of a market-based pricing system caused the price of domestic energy to be artificially low. Planners were effectively able to redistribute the value of oil and gas to other goods produced within the economy. The opportunity cost from sacrificing the export revenue from a barrel of oil in order for it to be used elsewhere in the production of goods with a much lower value represented a considerable subsidy to chronically inefficient Soviet enterprises. According to some estimates, the price of energy and power in the Soviet economy was as low as 5 per cent of world prices. This did little to encourage the conservation or efficient use of energy, making the Soviet Union one of the most energy-intensive countries in the world.

The surge in investment across resource-rich Siberia meant that, by the 1980s, the Soviet Union was the world's largest producer of oil and gas. The Soviet Union was able to maintain its role as a superpower in charge of a vast socialist empire, pay for an enormous military, and satisfy the basic needs of its population even as the planned economy lost its dynamism after the 1950s. However, this cemented the USSR's emergence as a type of 'petro power'. The share of oil and gas in total exports increased from 16 per cent in 1970 to 52 per cent in 1982. According to estimates by the economists Clifford Gaddy and Barry Ickes, oil revenues increased from just several billion dollars (in 2005 dollars) per year in the early 1970s to well over $260 billion per year by 1981.

There were a number of important consequences. It allowed the Soviet leadership to pursue its geopolitical competition with the West without having to address the systemic deficiencies within the economy that were causing productivity to decline. Indeed, the 1970s marked the height of Soviet military competition with the West. A blue-water navy was built, and the USSR achieved superiority over the United States in the number of strategic nuclear weapon systems that it was able to build and deploy. The Soviet Union also became increasingly active abroad, as shown by Soviet military interventions in the 1970s, first in Africa, and then in Afghanistan.

The military burden grew even as the underlying rate of productivity declined. According to one estimate, the share of military spending in Soviet output rose from an already exceptionally high 13 per cent in 1970 to at least 16 per cent in 1980. Such a colossal defence burden was only possible due to the enormous inflow of hydrocarbon revenues. But it also meant that the Soviet Union's position as one of the world's two superpowers rested on the income made from the sale of oil to its capitalist adversaries. This in turn meant that the fortunes of the socialist revolution were now dependent on the vicissitudes of the global economy.

As oil and gas production expanded, the Soviet Union became an increasingly important supplier of hydrocarbons to western Europe. The Soviet leadership used export revenues generated by oil and gas sales to purchase Western machinery and food. Over time, Western capitalist countries, and in particular those in western Europe, accounted for an increasingly large share of Soviet trade. In 1960, CMEA countries accounted for around 53 per cent of Soviet trade, but by 1980 their share had declined to 47 per cent. Over the same period, trade with the developed capitalist countries rose from less than 20 per cent of Soviet trade to over a third.

Imported advanced technologies from the West were not ideal from an ideological point of view. But they were intended by the leadership to regenerate the productive potential of the slowing Soviet economy and to help close the widening productivity gap between the Soviet Union and the West. Improving the technological base of production would, it was hoped, also lead to a corresponding improvement in the quality of consumer goods.

The USSR also imported increasing amounts of foodstuffs to mask the inability of the inefficient domestic agricultural sector to produce enough food to satisfy the consumption demands of the Soviet population. The Soviet Union, which in 1913 (as the Russian empire) was the largest exporter of grain in the world, became the world's largest importer in the 1980s, accounting for more than 15 per cent of the world's imported grain. While the Soviet Union was importing record volumes of agricultural produce from abroad it was also, through lower prices, subsidizing both the inefficient Soviet agricultural complex and the Soviet consumer. According to Yegor Gaidar, subsidies to the agricultural sector accounted for approximately a third of the state budget by the end of the 1980s.

By the early 1980s, productivity and economic growth more broadly continued to decline. By the time Brezhnev died in 1982, the Soviet Union had long been characterized by its own citizens as being in a state of *zastoi* (stagnation). Although a basic standard of living and social provision was available to most citizens, regardless of how productive they were, the gap between the Soviet Union and the capitalist West had ceased to close. Corruption rose as the 'stability of cadres' reduced the incentive for Soviet officials to govern in the public interest. What dynamism had existed in the system had almost disappeared. The widespread sense of hopeless inertia is perhaps best summed up by the Soviet joke that 'they pretend to pay us, and we pretend to work'.

This was not a good position for the world's second superpower to find itself in. Only the sale of oil and gas allowed the Soviet leadership to paper over the emerging cracks in the walls of the system. A range of different domestic groups within the Soviet system competed over access to export revenues: the military, client states, inefficient industries seeking subsidies, the war in Afghanistan, and so forth. Competing claims on the oil and gas windfall began to exceed revenues. Consequently, the depth of the Soviet Union's dependence on oil revenues left it painfully exposed to any decline in commodity prices.

It also left the USSR with an export profile that resembled an *un*developed state. It exported raw materials, rather than goods to which value had been added during the process of production, a point recognized within the top leadership. By facilitating the postponement of systemic reform, hydrocarbon revenues perpetuated the Soviet Union's backwardness. Most importantly, a state that aspired to a high level of self-sufficiency became increasingly exposed to the vagaries of the international economy due to its reliance on export earnings and the technology and consumer goods that these earnings enabled it to buy.

After the death of Brezhnev's successor, Yury Andropov, quickly followed by that of his successor, Konstantin Chernenko, it became increasingly apparent that reform of the system was necessary to inject renewed vigour into the economy. The new, young, and energetic General Secretary of the CPSU, Mikhail Gorbachev, appreciated the challenge facing the country. Upon acceding to the leadership, Gorbachev was bold enough to declare that the Soviet Union was in a 'pre-crisis situation'. Gorbachev was also quick to recognize the extent of the Soviet Union's hydrocarbon export dependence. Only three months after his election as General Secretary, he stated that the country should export more manufactured goods and fewer raw materials if the Soviet Union was to avoid finding itself in a position of 'inadmissible dependence' on the West.

Perestroika

Despite Gorbachev's apparent awareness of the weakness of the Soviet economy, which even official data revealed to be in seemingly inexorable decline, he did not initially embark on a campaign of systemic reform. Instead, his main policy innovations in 1986 were *uskorenie* (acceleration) and an anti-alcohol campaign designed to boost worker discipline. In this respect, his approach seemed to differ little from his mentor and predecessor, Yury Andropov. *Uskorenie*, which amounted to investing more in high-technology production while exhorting the labour force to work harder, displayed both a lack of imagination and the difficulty in reforming a system in which many incumbents were resistant to change.

It became quickly apparent that *uskorenie* would not deliver the results the leadership had hoped. Meanwhile, the prolonged, expensive, and unpopular war in Afghanistan, and the disastrous meltdown at the Chernobyl nuclear power plant in Ukraine, intensified the pressure on Gorbachev to overcome the mounting strains facing the CPSU. At this point the Soviet Union's excessive dependence on the global economy became apparent. In 1986, oil prices plummeted by nearly 70 per cent after Saudi Arabia decided dramatically to increase oil production. Total annual oil and gas revenues fell from a peak of over $260 billion in 1982 to just $75 billion in 1986. This restricted the options available to Gorbachev just at the point that he needed resources the most.

Dwindling hydrocarbon revenues meant that, unlike in the 1970s, when oil and gas exports concealed the weaknesses of the economy, systemic reform was the only route available to revive the economy. The decline in revenues added urgency to the reformist impulse, helping Gorbachev to persuade the CPSU that it needed to go further than it had ever gone before in addressing the deficiencies of the Soviet system. These reforms gradually became known as *perestroika*, or reconstruction.

The most important group of reforms from the perestroika period were the laws approved by the Soviet government granting increased independence for enterprises (the 1987 Law on State Enterprises, or LSE), and private economic activity (the 1988 Law on Cooperatives), which facilitated the legal creation of firms that were independent from state control.

In broad terms these reforms were intended to improve the incentives for Soviet workers and bosses. In doing so, it was hoped that they would become more productive. It was also hoped that the powerful and conservative industrial ministries which were seen as the main barriers to reform would be weakened as power flowed to the enterprises. The reforms were not intended to result in the construction of a free-market economy or the privatization of state property. Rather, the aim was to decentralize decision-making in the economy to weaken the ministries.

Meanwhile, it was hoped that some liberalization at the margin would improve economic performance without the CPSU having to relinquish political control.

The Law on State Enterprises was initially aimed at transferring power over enterprises from ministries to local party committees. A more decentralized form of 'self-management' that would still be consistent with the ideological precepts of the CPSU was envisaged. The main source of ministerial power, shared with Gosplan, had been their right to appoint enterprise managers, to decide production targets and investment plans, to set prices for goods, to allocate inputs, and to instruct enterprises where to deliver their output. The Law on State Enterprises eliminated many of these rights.

Enterprises now enjoyed the autonomy to make production decisions themselves, to choose their clients, set wages, and determine what proportion of profits would be retained. This should have effectively abolished central planning. However, under pressure from conservatives within the party and the ministries, the law also stipulated that enterprises should incorporate other instructions from the central authorities, thus giving the central planning authorities the formal power still to shape enterprise decision-making. This intensified the confusion over who controlled what. But importantly, the LSE removed accountability as a consideration for enterprise managers while simultaneously handing de facto ownership over to enterprise managers.

Meanwhile, the Law on Cooperatives legalized private enterprise among any group of more than three adults. Economic activity in these cooperatives would take place entirely outside any state direction or control. It was hoped that cooperatives would stimulate entrepreneurship that would in turn supply the demand for goods and services that the planned economy had hitherto been unable to achieve on its own.

It was envisaged that these cooperatives would then mobilize latent labour, providing competition to the state-owned enterprises, thereby forcing them to raise productivity. At least this was the intention. In practice, these economic reforms, alongside wider political reforms that took place at the same time, would fundamentally alter the manner in which workers and managers behaved, and in a manner that none of the architects of the reforms could have imagined.

The political component of perestroika was intended to galvanize the CPSU into becoming more responsive to the needs of the population. Gorbachev initiated a series of reforms that led to the introduction of limited elections to the Soviet legislature, first in each of the Soviet Union's constituent republics (e.g. Ukraine, Belarus, Russia, etc.) and then at the All-Union level. These elections were designed to generate greater accountability in the behaviour of party officials: if they did not perform and were not considered responsive to their constituents, they would be removed from office.

Taken together, the package of reforms collectively labelled as perestroika disturbed the delicate equilibrium in which the leadership and its citizens had coexisted since the 1930s. Enterprise directors possessed considerable informal power before 1985; however, the LSE gave this a legal basis. As a result, the power of the central authorities to monitor and manage enterprises was severely curtailed.

The constraints on enterprises were considerably reduced as perestroika effectively made property rights (hitherto held unambiguously by the state) increasingly ambiguous as the role of the central state receded. By creating the perception that Gosplan and ministry officials within the system were losing control over the management of state resources, enterprise directors became more opportunistic in utilizing the assets that were at their disposal. It was no longer clear who was ultimately in charge of the economy. As the confidence of enterprise directors grew, the credibility of the central Soviet authorities diminished further.

Catastroika

Within the economy, perestroika resulted in the emergence of 'spontaneous privatization' with enterprise managers tightening their control over state assets. Cooperatives were increasingly used not for private enterprise, but instead to appropriate state resources or to engage in speculation. The seizure of power and resources at lower levels was replicated in the political sphere as republics proclaimed their sovereignty against the centre.

The economic dimension of perestroika exacerbated the rush for power within the Soviet Union's constituent republics, such as Ukraine, Kazakhstan, Armenia, and, of course, Russia. This was because the LSE reduced the tax revenue raised by the central state as enterprises reduced payments. As the credibility of the Soviet centre to raise revenues declined, the republics withheld further transfers to Moscow as they focused on measures to rectify their own fiscal situations. Taken together, the Soviet state was subjected to the political equivalent of a bank run as the central Soviet authorities gradually saw their credibility undermined by the actions of local officials and enterprise directors responding opportunistically to earlier signs of weakness. The political and economic effects of this desertion by the party-state were disastrous, quickly leading to the collapse of the Soviet Union.

The economic impact was severe. Without the constraints previously put in place by the CPSU, enterprises began to pay their employees more. As enterprise directors withheld taxes, further pressure was put on the state budget. In order to fund the growing budget deficit, the Soviet authorities resorted to borrowing on international capital markets, and to printing money to cover the gap of lost revenues. This caused inflation to rise, something that had rarely occurred in the Soviet Union up to that point due to price and monetary controls.

With enterprise directors focused on short-term goals, investment plummeted by 7.4 per cent in 1988, and by a further 6.7 per cent in 1989. Soviet oil production also declined sharply after 1989, further intensifying the decline in state revenues even as prices began to rise again. Production declined from over 600 million metric tonnes per year in 1988 to around 500 million metric tonnes in 1990.

The economic collapse that ensued because of the failed policies of perestroika left the victorious Russian independence movement, led by the president, Boris Yeltsin (1931–2007), in control of a new state. However, the new Russian state was undermined by the very process that had brought it into existence. By ignoring the process of privatization from below in return for political support, the new Russian state repeated the same patterns of behaviour that existed under the Soviet state. This had the desired effect of undermining the collapsing Soviet state, but also laid the foundations for subsequent difficulties for the independent Russian state. Consequently, the state that later emerged from the wreckage of the Soviet Union inherited a severe economic crisis, as did the other newly independent republics.

The economic crisis of the late 1980s played a crucial role in bringing about the demise of the Soviet Union. Whether this collapse was inevitable will never be known. Had Gorbachev resisted the temptation to engage in systemic reform and instead preserved the core elements of the Stalinist system, perhaps the economy would have limped along until oil prices rose again, as they did in the 2000s when the Chinese economy re-entered the global economy. What is certain is that by removing much of the control of the CPSU over the economy, Gorbachev created the conditions for the republics to move towards independence. In doing so, they destroyed what for many of its citizens had been an oppressive and illegitimate system forged in a crucible of state-led violence that few countries have ever known.

Defenders of the Soviet Union's achievements point to the progress made in generating rapid industrialization and urbanization, and, in doing so, in equipping the Soviet Union with the tools to defeat Nazi Germany in the Great Patriotic War. The economic basis to support the emergence of the Soviet Union as a military superpower capable of competing with the world's largest economy, the United States, was also put in place. A comprehensive, if somewhat rudimentary, social welfare system was created. And mass employment was achieved. All this is true.

The price paid for these successes, however, was extreme. Millions of Soviet citizens died or suffered as state-led industrialization dragged a backward and agrarian economy into the industrialized 20th century. Individual initiative was stifled and fundamental freedoms denied. Throughout its entire existence, the Soviet system also displayed a remarkable indifference to the welfare of its citizenry, whether during the forced collectivization of the 1930s or in the reaction to the Chernobyl disaster in 1986. Consequently, when the Soviet Union disintegrated in relatively and surprisingly peaceful fashion at the end of 1991, many of its citizens hoped that a market-based economy would bring a freer and more prosperous future of a kind not witnessed before.

Chapter 3
The creation of a market

The Soviet Union was officially dissolved on 26 December 1991, although the newly independent Russian Federation had existed as a de facto state since August of that year. Boris Yeltsin, who was elected to the newly created Russian presidency in 1990, and who subsequently led Russia and the other Soviet republics to independence from the Soviet Union, was confronted now with the task of building institutions rather than destroying them.

Yeltsin faced the task of leading Russia through what many called a 'triple transition'. First, a new state and national identity needed to be built from the ashes of the now defunct Soviet state. Second, many hoped a democratic political system would replace the one-party authoritarian rule that defined the Soviet Union. Third, the planned economy, which had disintegrated so spectacularly at the end of Gorbachev's reign, was to be replaced with a market-based system. These challenges were not separate; progress in each, in some way, depended on success in the others.

The task of creating a market economy was, however, akin to rebuilding a ship at sea during a storm, with the conditions inherited from the end of the Soviet period imposing harsh constraints on the ambitious leadership of the new country. To this end, Yeltsin appointed a team of young reformers, led by the architect of economic reform in Russia, Yegor Gaidar (1956–2009).

However, the reformers were confronted by two sets of legacies of the Russian 'exit' from Soviet rule that made their job difficult: the first group economic in nature; and the second political.

The economy was in a state of crisis. Rampant inflation, onerous foreign debt obligations, a severe recession, a steep fall in investment, and dwindling tax revenues all meant that the new state had only minimal financial resources to begin the long job of building a new social order. In addition, the defection of the party-state apparatus in reaction to the failed reforms of perestroika meant that many state enterprises had been, or were in the process of being, appropriated by Soviet 'insiders'. This was a form of 'spontaneous' and illegal privatization. Furthermore, many inefficient enterprises employing millions of workers were in desperate need of reform. Under Soviet rule, these enterprises had effectively been reliant on the provision of soft budget constraints. Successful economic reform would entail altering the behaviour of these enterprises so that they would operate under hard budget constraints.

The breakdown of the Soviet planned economy also meant that trade between the ex-Soviet republics, something that had previously been a matter of internal economic management, was now a matter of external relations. Without orders from Gosplan providing demand for output from enterprises spread out across the former Soviet space, and without CPSU officials monitoring production, factories fell idle. Very few of the goods produced by these factories were competitive on global markets, leading to a rise in unemployment.

In the political sphere, Russia was emerging from a legacy of *patrimonial socialism* in which the political system combined elements of extreme repression, extensive networks of patron–client relations, and subtle competition among competing factions within the ruling elite. This meant that non-state forces in Russia were generally quite weak due to a legacy of repression and the limited availability of resources for organizations positioned outside state patronage networks. Because the state had been the source of patronage resources, the balance of political power in the newly independent states that emerged from patrimonial socialist systems was very often tilted in favour of those already wielding state authority.

In practice, this meant that access to the Soviet-era state patronage network was crucial to the acquisition of access to, or ownership of, state assets. In the late Soviet and early post-Soviet period, success in acquiring state assets, or in forming banks and other new economic organizations, usually involved accessing the state and long-standing patronage networks. The Soviet-era communist elite was best placed to benefit from both political and economic reform due to their ability to access resources that were unavailable to most other social groups. The activities of burgeoning political and economic organizations were focused on penetrating the state rather than building or co-opting strong, non-state organizations, such as those groups that form the liberal conception of civil society.

Together, these economic and political legacies—or 'initial conditions'—meant that the reformers faced staunch resistance from a number of directions. First, from the defeated but still influential supporters of the communist system who were determined to preserve the positions and privileges that they had enjoyed in the Soviet period. Second, from enterprise directors intent on acquiring the assets of the Soviet state for themselves. And, third, from a population that wanted an urgent end to the chaos and uncertainty caused by the collapse of socialism. These forms of resistance meant that the aspirations of reformers were quickly tempered by contact with political reality.

The need for reform

As the economic crisis caused by the failed reforms of the late Soviet period grew more severe, the ability of the new Russian state to implement policies was being weakened almost by the day. This was because the economy was in recession, state assets were being stolen, and firms were not paying taxes. Without a strong tax base, the state was unable to pay civil servants, law enforcement officers, and the army. Market reforms were seen as the only solution to the chaos that existed within the economy.

Different proposals to reform the economy were considered. So-called 'gradualists' proposed moving slowly away from the Soviet planned economy by removing subsidies and social welfare in a piecemeal fashion. This, it was believed, would retain the support of the population as a market was gradually built. By contrast, the proponents of what was called 'shock therapy' believed that a series of decisive reforms would quickly create the conditions for a market economy. The proponents of this policy also believed it would fatally weaken the former communist managers who remained in powerful positions. In the end, gradualism was rejected as a strategy because of the scarcity of resources available to the government. There was simply not enough money available to continue paying for the vast range of subsidies and commitments that the Russian government was obliged to provide.

The economic reform plan devised by Gaidar's team at the end of 1991 was designed to reduce the role of the state in many areas of the economy. Gaidar referred to this as 'taming the state', which had always been so dominant throughout Russian history, both during the communist period and before. This was to be achieved by drastically cutting subsidies to Soviet-era enterprises and imposing hard budget constraints. It was hoped that this would reduce the financial burden on the state. Broadly, the reform plan comprised three core elements.

First, the government hoped to achieve macroeconomic stabilization. This involved securing macroeconomic balance as quickly as possible in the hope that this would reduce inflation and create the conditions for a new currency. To do this required disciplined monetary and fiscal policies. Interest rates were to be high and strict limits were put in place on the creation of money. It was hoped that this would reduce inflationary pressures within the economy. Alongside this, a tight fiscal policy required the government to slash spending on the military, industrial subsidies, and social welfare payments. Taxes were also raised.

Second, the rules that had tightly controlled economic activity in the Soviet Union were to be liberalized. Domestic liberalization involved removing administrative constraints on economic activity and permitting markets to function. New companies were able to emerge and to trade freely. Liberalization also involved lifting the controls over the prices of goods and services. Whereas bureaucrats set prices in the planned economy, markets and the balance between supply and demand would set them in Russia. It was envisaged that the liberalization of prices would have the effect of improving the incentives for enterprises to be profitable (by allowing the price mechanism to reflect supply and demand) and thereby shift production away from value-subtracting activities to areas that that would be more beneficial to the economy. External liberalization removed barriers to foreign trade, reducing customs duties and permitting enterprises to establish links with firms from across the world. Over time, reformers also planned to move towards full currency convertibility.

Third, the government acknowledged the need to privatize state-owned assets quickly. For as long as state bureaucrats retained control over large economic resources, reformers feared that they would have little incentive to increase efficiency and move away from seeking soft budget constraints. Politically, privatization was seen as perhaps the most important reform of them all. By overturning state ownership of the means of production, it was hoped that the social and economic basis for a return of the communists would be eliminated. Doing this, however, was complicated. For example, it was difficult to know who should become the new owners. Should existing management be given ownership of their factories? Or should shares in factories be given to the general population? And what role was to be played by foreign owners? Should large Western conglomerates, for example, be allowed to own and run Russia's strategically important oil and gas fields? There were no clear answers to these questions.

One of Gaidar's most capable colleagues, Anatoly Chubais, was put in charge of managing this complex and politically charged process. This task was seen as especially urgent due to the spontaneous and illegal privatization of state assets that had been taking place since perestroika. After some deliberation, and under pressure from powerful industrialists, Chubais embarked on a dual strategy. First, he allowed management and employees to buy a proportion of the shares in the enterprises they managed. This satisfied the most vocal complaints emanating from industrialists. Second, privatization vouchers were issued to the whole population. These could be traded freely and gave citizens the chance to own shares in Russia's sprawling network of enterprises. This led Yeltsin in the summer of 1992 to describe voucher privatization as 'people's capitalism'.

If successful, these reforms were intended to cause a sudden and sharp change in the distribution of resources within the Russian economy. The Soviet party-state elite (who would have to restructure and become profitable to survive) would either change or disappear, while new economic actors would materialize in response to the changing incentive structure. In short, communists would vanish and capitalists would replace them. The economic influence of a newly configured and 'tamed' state would be curtailed considerably, leaving it to manage a much smaller spending bill, and to control the money supply and provide price stability. Over time, the state would then gradually become stronger as taxation revenues from a growing economy rose. The privatization of state assets would further increase the incentive amongst enterprises to become profitable. This would have the added political advantage of further reducing the influence of the Soviet party-state elite. Or so the theory went. In practice, these reforms proved painful and generated immediate resistance from a wide range of social groups.

Painful reform

Macroeconomic stabilization led to savage cuts in government spending. Spending on defence, which had already been cut severely by Gorbachev, was cut by a further 80 per cent in the government's first budget for 1992. Procurement of weapons and equipment from Russia's vast defence-industrial complex ground to a near halt. Wages and privileges for the military were cut. Industrial subsidies followed suit, leaving giant, uncompetitive enterprises unable to pay workers. The government and the central bank, for the first half of 1992 at least, were able to resist calls for an expansion of credit and the resumption of subsidies. As a result, macroeconomic balance seemed in reach: the budget deficit narrowed and inflation declined. However, as wages declined and unemployment grew, government discipline began to weaken.

Liberalization proved just as challenging. Numerous opportunities were created by the removal of barriers to trade. Kiosks and market stalls sprang up across Russia's towns and cities. Imported goods appeared on the shelves of shops where previously they had been empty. A whole range of goods and services that never existed under socialism were now available to those who could afford them. This offered opportunities for entrepreneurs to make substantial profits.

Price liberalization, however, was painful. On 2 January 1992, price controls for 90 per cent of consumer goods were removed. Reformers saw this as desirable. They knew that if prices for scarce goods increased sharply, the incentive for entrepreneurs to supply those goods would rise. As the supply of those goods expanded, the price would gradually fall over time. The reformers therefore expected an initial spike in inflation, but were confident that this would decline as other reforms took effect.

In January, the rate of monthly inflation reached 225 per cent. Savings that were accumulated by citizens during the Soviet period, when there were not enough goods in the shops to spend their wages on, were suddenly used to chase the small volume of previously unavailable goods. But as the year went on, the disciplined fiscal and monetary policies of the reformist government helped ensure that inflation declined. More goods appeared on shelves and by May monthly inflation had dropped to 45 per cent. This was still high, but it showed that government policies were beginning to work.

Unfortunately, Gaidar's team was not given the breathing space to implement its policies. Public dissatisfaction with high inflation and rising unemployment rose sharply. Reforms were also challenged by the representatives of the Soviet party-state elite in the parliament (the Soviet-era Congress of Peoples' Deputies). The most vocal resistance came from Civic Union, led by Arkady Volsky. Civic Union brought together a range of different interest groups, including industrialists. The government's reforms threatened them with destruction. They were particularly concerned by the scarcity of capital due to the reformists' disciplined monetary policy. Without access to credit, they argued, the prospects for an investment-led restructuring process were bleak.

The industrial resistance to reform took two forms. First, on the formal, national level, the government was lobbied by groups within parliament to ease monetary discipline and to raise government expenditure, most notably on industrial subsidies. Second, on an informal and subnational level, enterprises, particularly those appropriated or managed by the Soviet party-state elite, simply carried on operating as they had under

Soviet rule. They placed orders with other firms for goods and services, and those firms in turn placed orders with them. In the absence of capital—through access to credit or generated by profits—these firms 'paid' for goods either in kind (through barter exchange) or by building up debts with each other (inter-enterprise debts). The government was even complicit in this arrangement as it helped keep unemployment, and social discontent more generally, lower than it would otherwise have been. This became known as the 'virtual economy', and its existence revealed the extent to which reform was failing to change the behaviour of the Soviet-era party-state elite.

By the second half of 1992, under intense pressure, the government and central bank began to relax the previously tough monetary and budgetary policies. Subsidies rose and credit was extended to ailing enterprises. This caused the money supply to rise, which in turn led to inflation rising again by the end of the year. While wages were paid and some received pay rises, inflation rose faster, causing real incomes to decline further. Just as the government's tough policies were paying off, it was forced to retreat. While liberalization was largely successful, macroeconomic stability would prove much harder to achieve. A pattern of policy 'zigzagging' emerged over the 1990s: tough policies would be implemented, only to be reversed under pressure from industrialists and the population. New measures would then later be devised, but would also be reversed under pressure. It soon became apparent that politics made economic reform very difficult to implement in practice.

Privatization

Meanwhile, privatization generated its own controversies. While a few well-placed insiders—usually members of the Soviet party-state elite—enjoyed rapid enrichment, for most voucher privatization was viewed as a sham. Individual citizens were in no position to stop the vast majority of factory managers from seizing full control of their enterprises. Within a few months of vouchers being issued to the population at the end of 1992 they were worthless to most people. In some instances, voucher investment funds emerged to manage people's investments. However, a series of widely publicized scams and pyramid schemes eroded people's confidence in the whole process. The Russian word *prikhvatization* entered the parlance, implying that privatization was merely a cover for theft.

Public confidence in privatization sagged further with the so-called 'loans for shares' episode in 1995. Prior to the 1996 presidential election, it looked certain that it would be won by the Communist Party of the Russian Federation candidate, Gennady Zyuganov. To prevent this, Chubais and others in the Yeltsin administration arranged for the government to borrow money from several of the richest businessmen in the country. In return for these loans and political support against his communist opponents, a convoluted scheme was devised that ultimately resulted in the sale of valuable state assets—particularly in the natural resource sector—to domestic financiers and industrialists at what many believed were knock-down prices.

A substantial portion of the oil industry was privatized in this manner, along with much of the metallurgical sector. One of the businessmen, Mikhail Khodorkovsky, was able to turn his newly acquired oil company, Yukos, into one of the world's largest corporations by the early 2000s, and, in doing so, become Russia's richest person. Yeltsin won the subsequent election by the skin of his teeth (and with the help of a lot of electoral fraud), but the loans for shares episode came to represent the worst excesses of economic change in Russia's 'wild east' (Figure 1).

Later, some suggested that the loans for shares arrangement created a class of hugely influential so-called 'oligarchs'. This, however, is inaccurate. The fact that a group of businessmen were in a position to lend money to, and quite possibly swindle, the

1. Yeltsin with powerful industrialists.

government of a former superpower in the first place showed that they were already rich and powerful. Instead, loans for shares involved only a small number of a larger group of super-rich businessmen that emerged in the early 1990s. They did so largely by taking advantage of the opportunities created by economic reform. Many, although not all, of these oligarchs were former members of the Soviet party-state elite. Only a few 'outsiders', such as Boris Berezovsky and Vladimir Guisinsky, were able to join this group without the advantages bestowed by links to the Soviet apparatus. But most of these oligarchs were savvy insiders who were able to turn Soviet power into money in the new Russia.

The social price of reform

If the government found economic transformation difficult to manage, the majority of the population found it even harder. While official statistics suggested unemployment was not as high as some feared—fluctuating between 10 and 12 per cent—this concealed the real truth (Table 2). Due to the slump in industry, enterprises kept workers on their books even if they only turned up occasionally or went largely unpaid. Employees agreed to this arrangement because enterprises continued to provide a range of social services, such as health care or holidays, as they had during the Soviet period. Therefore, *underemployment* was much higher than unemployment.

Wages were often unpaid or, at best, paid in arrears. The real value of those wages that were paid was relentlessly eroded by inflation. This also affected pensions and other forms of social welfare. Inequality surged as a small number of people, often Soviet-era insiders or criminals, became fantastically rich while the majority of ordinary people saw their living standards plummet. Savings were wiped out and people were forced to sell their belongings. Many of those that could leave left the country. Crime rose spectacularly. As the huge army was cut in the early 1990s, large numbers of ex-military servicemen, skilled in the application of violence, found themselves working in the private sector as guards or enforcers for the newly rich or criminal groups. The underpaid and under-resourced police were often no match for criminal groups. The murder rate climbed throughout the 1990s and the sense of lawlessness rose. While Russia was a much freer country in the 1990s, the number of those who were able to enjoy these new freedoms and the prosperity that many hoped would go with them was rather small. For a large number of Russian citizens, reform and the end of the Soviet Union was associated with chaos, disorder, and a decline in living standards that was far more severe than that experienced by the United States during the Great Depression.

A price worth paying?

By the mid-1990s, reformers had succeeded in laying some of the foundations of a market economy. Restrictions on economic activity were liberalized. Price controls were lifted. And chronic shortages of goods in the shops came to an end. The burden of

Table 2. Key indicators of economic performance, 1992–99

	1992	1993	1994	1995	1996	1997	1998	1999
GDP, %-change	−14.5	−8.7	−12.7	−4.1	−3.6	1.4	−5.3	6.4
GDP, USD billion		183	274	313	384	404	269	196
Industrial production, %-change y-o-y	−16.0	−13.7	−21.6	−4.6	−7.6	1.0	−4.8	8.0
Fixed investments, %-change y-o-y	−39.7	−11.7	−24.3	−10.1	−18.1	−5.0	−12.0	5.3
Retail sales, %-change y-o-y	0.3	1.6	0.2	−6.2	0.3	4.9	−3.2	−5.8
Exports, USD billion			66.1	81.1	88.5	85.9	73.7	69.7
Imports, USD billion			48.1	60.8	67.6	71.7	57.5	37.3
Unemployment, %	5.2	5.9	8.1	9.4	9.7	11.8	13.3	13.0
Inflation, %, y-o-y		874.3	307.7	197.4	47.8	14.8	27.7	85.8
Federal government balance, % of GDP		−5.8	−10.0	−3.0	−3.7	−3.7	−3.3	−1.1
Central government debt, % of GDP		70.1	57.6	49.8	50.8	54.4	71.0	79.0
External debt, % of GDP		61.0	43.2	36.6	32.7	33.4	50.8	67.0
External debt, USD billion		111.8	118.5	114.8	125.8	135.2	136.5	131.2

Source: Bank of Finland Institute for Economies in Transition (from official Russian sources).

militarization, which had weighed down the Soviet economy, was also much reduced. By the end of the 1990s, over 60 per cent of the economy was in private hands. The state ownership of the means of production had been much diminished, stifling the chances of a communist return to power. These were vital elements of a market economy and remain in place today. Indeed, when taking a long view over the five centuries or so of Russia's existence, it is fair to say that the reforms of the 1990s caused the market to be stronger than at any point in Russian history.

Unfortunately, these successes came at the expense of a large number of important compromises which, for many, would forever taint the way in which reforms were perceived. Perhaps most importantly, in an effort to keep a grip on power in the face of a resurgent communist party, Yeltsin and his inner circle ensured that lucrative state assets were transferred to his supporters, both during the period of mass privatization in the early 1990s and then, in a more high-profile fashion, during the loans for shares episode in 1995. While this enabled Yeltsin to cling on to power, the legitimacy of economic reform in the eyes of a significant proportion of the population was sacrificed to make this happen.

The slow pace of restructuring

Despite the tumultuous economic change that took place in the 1990s, the Russian economy experienced only limited structural change. Enterprises were not investing in new factories and machinery. Instead, billions of dollars' worth of private capital was leaving Russia every year. The perception, and indeed reality, of lawlessness and chaos was clearly a major factor in discouraging investment. This sentiment was shared by foreign investors with foreign direct investment (FDI) into Russia very low, particularly when compared with other countries of the post-socialist region. What FDI did make its way into Russia was mostly concentrated

The creation of a market

in the natural resources sector and did not visibly improve the everyday life of Russian citizens.

This absence of investment—both domestic and foreign—resulted in the preservation of much of the Soviet-era production structure. To be sure, many of the older, inefficient enterprises vanished. Those that were not politically influential, in the textiles industry for example, went bust and disappeared. Small- and medium-sized enterprises (SMEs) also emerged. Unfortunately, the same factors that suppressed investment elsewhere in the economy—poor business environment, weak property rights, etc.—caused them to grow at a much slower rate than reformers had hoped. Whereas SMEs typically account for around two-thirds of employment in developed economies, in the mid-1990s legally registered SMEs in Russia accounted for less than 10 per cent of employment. Companies in consumer industries (e.g. food processing, breweries, furniture producers, etc.) performed especially well. By contrast, large firms employing over 500 workers accounted for nearly two-thirds of official employment in 1996. Many of these were the larger, politically influential 'dinosaur' enterprises that were able to survive through a combination of subsidies and credits. As a result, by the late 1990s, Russia's economic structure resembled that of the Soviet Union.

Low investment and structural transformation meant that the role of the oil and gas sectors remained of central importance to the Russian economy. Russia remained a petro-state, albeit one that was producing much smaller volumes than during the Soviet period. In 1997, eleven out of the twenty-five largest companies by market capitalization in Russia were involved in the oil and gas sector. As the most profitable sectors in the economy, close links quickly developed between the state and the largest oil and gas firms. This was perhaps natural given that they constituted the largest sector in the Russian economy, and that oil and gas export earnings were the most important source of taxation revenue, accounting for around 40 per cent of budget receipts during this period. These sectors were particularly important as they offered a source of revenue that badly performing enterprises within the virtual economy could not. Large swathes of the rest of the economy remained dependent on the redistribution of profits made in oil and gas to keep them afloat.

The August 1998 financial crisis

After narrowly winning the presidential election in 1996, Yeltsin then presided over Russia's first year of positive growth (1.4 per cent) in gross domestic product (GDP) in 1997. After suffering a long and severe recession, many hoped that this return to growth might signal happier times for Russia's long-suffering population. This proved to be a mirage. Even during 1997, the benefits of modest growth were mostly felt in the large cities, especially Moscow. Many of the fundamental problems afflicting the Russian economy remained unsolved.

The government remained unable to balance expenditure and revenues. Large businesses proved adept at evading tax payments, while the existence of the 'virtual economy'—the large swathe of Russian industry that refused to restructure and behave like profit-seeking enterprises—made tax collection even more difficult. Yet government spending continued to exceed its low revenues. Something needed to be done, so in an effort to bridge the gap between state income and expenditure, the government began to issue high-interest-bearing short-term state bonds (GKOs) as a non-inflationary way of funding the budget deficit. As with the shares for loans arrangement, the major beneficiaries were the big Russian banks owned by the very same businessmen who were evading tax payments through their other businesses.

In 1997, the Russian government opened up its debt market to foreign investors, leading to rapid inflows of foreign capital. Indeed, these inflows were the primary reason for the growth of GDP in that year. However, the Asian financial crisis of 1997 soon spread to other emerging market economies. This caused a 'flight to safety' among foreign investors and the sudden withdrawal of short-term capital from Russia. At the same time, the weakening of global demand for commodities caused by the slump across Asia resulted in a steep drop in oil prices. Russia's dependence on oil revenues struck again, only it was now amplified by the fact that the government had built up a large stock of expensive debt. Russia was plunged into crisis as the state defaulted on much of its domestic debt and the private sector defaulted on its foreign debt. This led to panic on international capital markets, a collapse of confidence in the Russian banking sector, and the devaluation of the rouble. That year, GDP fell by 5.3 per cent and unemployment rose again, reaching an official peak of 13.3 per cent.

It seemed at this point as though economic reform in Russia had failed. What was once the world's second superpower was now a country on its knees. The attempt to build a market economy seemed to have created problems as severe as those found in the Soviet economy. During the Soviet period, people had jobs and money, but would struggle to find the goods to spend it on. In the 1990s, by contrast, all manner of goods and services were available. But very few people had the jobs or money to afford them. The market reforms appeared to be yet another episode of extreme turbulence in Russia's long and often painful history. The communist party enjoyed a surge in approval and hard-fought reforms looked to be under threat.

The aftermath of the crisis

After the 1998 financial crisis wiped out the wealth of many of Russia's fledgling middle class, the public began to demand the reassertion of law and order. A former director of Soviet foreign intelligence, Yevgeny Primakov, was appointed prime minister with the support of the communists in parliament. With presidential elections scheduled for 2000, and popular support for market reforms ebbing away, it seemed only a matter of time before a communist would take the all-powerful presidency.

Instead a little-known ex-KGB officer, Vladimir Putin, was appointed first as prime minister in the summer of 1999, and then as acting president on the eve of the millennium. This came as the economy made a surprise return to rapid growth: GDP expanded by 6.5 per cent in 1999 and unemployment began to drop. A stronger economy helped boost support for the new man in the Kremlin. Mr Putin promised to restore what the Russians called *poryadok*, or order, and to rein in the power of big business. He declared himself a *liberal derzhavnik*, which roughly translates as a man that believes in Russia as a liberal but strong state. There was, though, an obvious tension: if the state became stronger, what would happen to the market freedoms that had been so painfully won since Mikhail Gorbachev had initiated perestroika over a decade before?

Chapter 4
The reassertion of the state

Vladimir Putin was appointed as acting prime minister on 9 August 1999. On the same day, Islamist fighters from Chechnya, a restive region in Russia's north Caucasus, entered neighbouring Dagestan, another region of Russia. In response, one of Putin's first actions was to oversee a large-scale military campaign to assert Moscow's rule in the region. The new prime minister's actions followed a bloody and unpopular war in Chechnya that had only ended a few years before. This time, however, the war was fought more successfully. Against the backdrop of improving economic fortunes, Mr Putin quickly became the most popular politician in Russia. The popularity of Putin prompted the president, Boris Yeltsin, to announce his resignation in dramatic style on 31 December. In doing so, Yeltsin made Putin acting president and created the conditions for what became an overwhelming win at the polls in March 2000.

At the time, very little was known about Putin. Even less was known about his views on the economy. There was speculation about whether he would continue with the difficult market reforms of the 1990s, or would instead choose to reassert the role of the state in the Russian economy. The latter, after all, had dominated economic development for most of its history. Clues to Mr Putin's thinking were contained in the 'millennium manifesto', mentioned at the beginning of this book. The manifesto gave clues as to Putin's views on a wide range of issues, including his vision of the country's future economic development.

In the article Putin bemoaned the poor state of the economy. He highlighted Russia's comparatively small economy, the low levels of per capita income and productivity, and the overdependence of the economy on natural resources. He also lamented the poor state of the country's technological capabilities and a severe decline in health, law and order, and the overall quality of life. It was a frank and honest assessment of where Russia found itself on the eve of the millennium. But Putin did not blame the painful and only partially successful market reforms of the 1990s. Instead he argued that Russia's weaknesses were 'inherited from the Soviet Union'. To be sure, policymakers had made 'mistakes and miscalculations'. But, he argued, there was 'no alternative' to the market. The only question was: how to make 'market mechanisms work to full capacity'.

Putin proposed a three-pronged strategy to rejuvenate the country. First, a 'Russian idea' was needed. This meant that Russia needed to bind its population around an identity that fused the best of Russia's old traditions with renewed 'belief in the greatness of Russia'. Second, he argued that Russia needed a strong state, which, he argued, was the 'guarantor of order and the initiator and main driving force of any change'. This was needed to reassert control over Russia's far-flung and sometimes restive regions, and to launch an 'offensive on crime'. Third, Putin outlined a series of measures to improve the functioning of the market. He highlighted the need to increase the rate of investment, from both domestic and foreign sources, to improve industrial policy to promote high-technology industries, and to accelerate Russia's integration with the global economy. These themes would recur throughout his time in office.

But at the beginning of 2000 it was unclear how Putin would combine these ambitions. Building a strong state and a market are not necessarily mutually exclusive goals. Indeed, all successful markets across the world are embedded in well-functioning states. However, achieving a healthy balance between the two had not happened in Russia before. Consequently, there was a fear that if Putin strengthened the state it would come at the expense of the newly won market freedoms.

The restoration of order

Like Yeltsin in 1990, Vladimir Putin began his reign as Russian president in 2000 with overwhelming popular support. It seemed he had a window of opportunity to reignite economic reform, especially as he spent his early days in office speaking enthusiastically about the need to develop a society based on the rule of law. The potential to achieve this was greater in the aftermath of the August 1998 crisis. The power of big business had been weakened with the collapse of much of the Russian banking system, and the virtual economy had declined in size. Both of these changes were a direct consequence of the financial crisis.

Initially, the reassertion of the state under Putin was focused on two areas. First, Putin concentrated on reining in regional bosses by reforming Russia's federal structure. Instead of allowing Russia's eighty-nine different regions to effectively rule themselves as they had under Yeltsin, he created seven 'super regions'. These were headed by officials loyal to Putin and they tightened Moscow's grip on Russia's regions. This represented another blow to big business as they had often aligned themselves with regional elites against federal authority. Both business and regional elites were now encouraged to work with Putin and organizations loyal to him.

Putin then went on the offensive against two of the most prominent of the so-called oligarchs: Boris Berezovsky and Vladimir Gusinsky. Using formal bankruptcy proceedings, both were stripped of their major business interests in Russia, including the two important independent media groups, as well as other industrial assets. Both fled the country. It was the first time that a newly drafted bankruptcy law had been used to 'deprivatize' assets owned by powerful businessmen. It would not be the last, and represented a clear shift in the balance of power between the business and the state.

Nevertheless, despite the fates of Berezovsky and Gusinsky, many saw the redistribution of power between business and state as much needed. After all, in the eyes of many, these plutocrats had exercised too much power in the 1990s. Now that a healthy level of respect between state and business had been established, there appeared to be a greater chance than ever of moving towards a better functioning market and polity.

In the summer of 2000, this was followed by the so-called *shashlychnoe sogleshenie* (the 'shashlik agreement'). Here, it was alleged, Putin met with other powerful business leaders over a lavish barbecue held outside Moscow. Putin was reported to have told them that if they stayed out of politics and paid their taxes, he would allow them to keep their businesses. The implication was that if they did not do this, their property and liberty would be at risk.

An expanding and stable economy

It was clear that Putin possessed the will and ability to follow through on his promise to strengthen the state. However, he also revealed a reform agenda, produced at the end of 1999 by the Centre for Strategic Research, a liberal-minded think tank headed by Putin's personal friend German Gref, who was appointed as minister of the economy. Over the next three years, Putin and his government, including economic liberals like finance minister Alexei Kudrin, implemented a number of measures from what was labelled the 'Gref Plan'. Over this period, the government introduced a 13 per cent flat tax, which was considered an innovative and path-breaking step at the time. Along with rising oil prices, it quickly helped boost tax revenues. Corporation tax was reduced, while public utilities, including the cumbersome electricity industry, and land laws were reformed.

These reforms appeared to yield almost immediate rewards. Macroeconomic stability, which had proven so elusive under Yeltsin, was quickly achieved, with Russia achieving a budget surplus in 2001 for the first time. The government used these surpluses to pay down Russia's stock of sovereign debt that grew in the 1990s. Government external debt declined from $131 billion at the end of 1999 to less than $40 billion in 2007. At just 3 per cent of GDP, state external debt was now among the lowest in the world. Budget surpluses grew so much that a stabilization fund was created in 2004 where surplus tax revenues were accumulated. Annual inflation dropped from 85 per cent in 1999 to just 15 per cent in 2002. Most importantly, GDP continued to expand at an average annual rate of just under 7 per cent between 1999 and 2004. Living standards rose, and the memories of the chaos and poverty of the 1990s began to recede.

In the political sphere, economic growth and the accompanying influx of tax revenues increased the relative power of the state. Unlike Yeltsin, Putin was not reliant either on loans or favours from business, and did not need to parcel out state property to shore up his political position. Within just a few years, Putin appeared to have repaired much of the damage that had left the Russian state in such a weak position in 1998. His apparent commitment to prudent fiscal and monetary policies played a crucial role in making this possible.

Sources of growth

Was this reversal of fortunes down to Putin's good planning, or was he simply lucky? It was probably a combination of both. Global oil prices, which rose due to the war in Iraq and because of the rapidly growing Chinese economy's appetite for raw materials, certainly helped. Oil production, which had declined amidst the chaos of the 1990s, also grew briskly. Rising prices and the expansion of oil production caused a rapid and sustained rise in oil and gas revenues, which boosted the wider economy (Figure 2). The weakness of the rouble also helped. It had depreciated sharply after the financial crisis, and this meant that goods produced in Russia were now cheaper than those produced abroad. Many Russians switched to buying home-grown products, boosting demand for local production. And importantly, the institutional reforms carried out under Yeltsin were finally paying off. Now that macroeconomic stability had been achieved, the fruits of liberalization and privatization were finally harvested.

Nevertheless, considerable credit has to be given to Putin and the government he appointed to manage the economy. They resisted the temptation to give away these windfall resources to politically and socially powerful groups, such as the military. Spending the windfall would have been easy to do and would have proven very popular. However, military spending as a proportion of GDP declined during this period. Subsidies to industry also declined. Russia's fiscal and monetary policies were now the envy of the

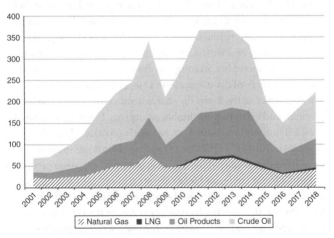

2. **Oil and gas export revenues, 2001–18 (constant 2015 USD, billion).**

world. This took political courage and was in stark contrast to economic policy under Yeltsin.

The Yukos affair

As global oil prices rose, and as the now largely privatized Russian oil industry pumped greater volumes, the political importance of Russia's oil and gas revenues grew. Although tax revenues from the non-oil economy had risen at a rapid rate, oil and gas were still the most lucrative sectors. As a result, the incentive for the state to tax and control the oil and gas sectors was very high. In 2000, Putin had already moved to reassert control over Gazprom, the gas-producing behemoth that descended directly from the Soviet Ministry of Gas. But the oil industry was largely in private hands and yielded higher tax revenues than gas. The cost of losing control over the oil industry's earnings was potentially very high.

What would become the defining moment for Russia's oil industry, and perhaps even for the wider system of political economy, came in 2003. While most so-called oligarchs had abided by the terms of the 'shashlik agreement' of July 2000, one stood out for maintaining an independent and decidedly political approach to running his business. Mikhail Khodorkovsky, the owner of Yukos, was Russia's richest person (Figure 3). He had successfully turned his oil company from a badly run entity that was on the verge of disintegration in 1995 (until acquired by Khodorkovsky in the loans for shares arrangement) to a modern, efficient, and extremely profitable enterprise. In doing so, he had involved himself in a number of political activities. He paid deputies in Russia's parliament (the State Duma) to support legislation that favoured his business interests, exposed corruption in Putin's inner circle, and was very open about his future political ambitions. Khodorkovsky also began negotiations to sell Yukos to ExxonMobil, threatening to shift control over Russia's largest oil fields to foreign owners. Together, these were unacceptable to Putin and the ruling elite.

3. Vladimir Putin speaking with Mikhail Khodorkovsky in the Kremlin in 2001.

Putin moved decisively in October 2003 when Khodorkovsky was arrested on charges of tax fraud. He was tried in 2004, jailed for ten years, and only released in 2013. Khodorkovsky ceased to be a political threat, sending a powerful signal to any other powerful businessman with pretensions to political power. The main oil-producing arm within Yukos was surreptitiously transferred to the state-owned company Rosneft. Prior to this, Rosneft was a small and insignificant company. But it was now a major player and would become Russia's largest oil company run by one of the country's most powerful men, Igor Sechin. For many observers, especially outside Russia, the Yukos affair revealed Putin's commitment to the market and the rule of law to be shallow. Within Russia, few sympathized with Khodorkovsky, due to the general population's largely jaundiced view of how he had acquired his immense wealth.

The expansion of the state

Yukos proved to be a watershed moment. It was followed by a series of other state acquisitions of private property, not least the transfer of Roman Abramovich's Sibneft to the state-controlled Gazprom in October 2005. Abramovich had studiously stayed out of politics. As a result, he received $13.1 billion for the sale and used his money to, among other things, bankroll Chelsea Football Club. The contrast with Khodorkovsky was glaring. Play by Putin's rules and life could be very comfortable. Disobey them and you would lose everything.

Foreign investors also saw their role in the oil sector weakened. Royal Dutch-Shell's participation in energy projects on and near the island of Sakhalin in Russia's Far East was restricted when it was forced to cede majority ownership of the Sakhalin 2 joint venture to Gazprom. This was followed by TNK-BP's forced sale of its majority share of the licence to develop the Kovytka gas field. By 2007, only Surgutneftegaz and Lukoil remained as significant private oil companies. The rest were owned or controlled by the state. The state also increased its control over other 'strategic' sectors in Russia's mining and armaments industries.

After 2005, a number of state corporations (*goskorporatsii*) were formed. These were giant industrial entities formed through the consolidation of disparate enterprises across different industries considered to be of strategic importance to the ruling elite. One of the largest was Rostec (Russian Technologies), a sprawling collection of manufacturing firms, many of which produced military equipment. State corporations were owned and managed by public officials, heralding a new phase in business–state relations. Where business had been dominant in the 1990s, now the state—through direct ownership, representation on company management boards, or through the implicit threat of legal action—was able to exert considerable control over economic activity. The chaos of the market in the 1990s had given way to a more state-directed model of economic management. Much had changed in Russia's economy due to the reforms of the 1990s, but, it seemed, even more had stayed the same.

The Putinist model of political economy

What emerged during Putin's first two terms as president (2000–8) was neither a market- nor a state-controlled economy. Instead, it was a more complex hybrid system of political economy that balanced the needs of different segments of society. Within this system, pockets of relative freedom and competition coexisted alongside large swathes of the economy where the state was dominant and competition was restricted. It is possible to present a simplified picture of the system that emerged under Putin in which the Russian economy is divided into three parts.

The first part—'Sector A'—is largely made up of enterprises from the oil, gas, and mining sectors, as well as some large agricultural corporations, and businesses involved in the construction of armaments and machinery for generating nuclear power. Firms in this sector are globally competitive as they sell their goods or services on global markets as well as within Russia. They do not require state subsidies to survive. The state is dominant in these sectors, either through direct ownership (oil, gas, nuclear, defence) or through strong influence over privately owned firms (mining, agriculture).

A second part—'Sector B'—encompasses industries that are not globally competitive because these firms do not sell their goods or services on global markets. Instead, they focus on the domestic Russian market. These firms tend to rely on subsidies or other forms of support from the state, which either transfers resources to them or shields them from competition. Despite receiving this kind of support from the state, these firms often struggle to make profits. These industries include parts of the defence industry, the car industry, and shipbuilding. As well as industrial sectors, Sector B comprises social groups dependent on the state for their income. These are the so-called *byudzhetniki*, or people dependent on budget transfers. These include pensioners and civil servants.

The links between these two broad sectors explain much of how Russian political economy works. Much of the profit made in Sector A is taken by the state and redistributed to Sector B. This is done for a number of economic, social, and political reasons. But the state's role is crucial and it is able to use a number of methods to do this. The most obvious mechanism is to tax the profits in Sector A and then spend it on orders for goods from Sector B, or to increase pensions or salaries in the civil service. Or the state might exert informal power over privately owned firms to 'encourage' them to perform social or political functions that would not normally be expected of a firm in a market economy. Taken together, these methods enable the state to support production and employment in otherwise uncompetitive areas of the Russian economy. This keeps people in work and boosts incomes.

One of the important features of this system is that the state uses state-owned enterprises (SOEs) as instruments of governance. Very often, Russian SOEs pursue objectives beyond that of simply making a profit for the main shareholder, that is, the state. Instead, these firms are often required to perform functions that promote social and regional development. Sometimes they are used to advance the foreign policy objectives of the Kremlin. Another characteristic of this system is that the strength of property rights is, in practice if not in law, conditional upon close relations with government officials. This is especially the case in the lucrative and strategically important natural resources sector, as shown in the Khodorkovsky affair.

Competition in both sectors is suppressed by the state. This can take the form of legal barriers to the emergence of new firms, or financial support for incumbents. Economic efficiency—that is, the requirement of profitability—is not required to guarantee firms' survival within these sectors. Instead, as in the Soviet period, budget constraints for these firms tended to be soft. What is often more important to a firm's survival prospects is whether the firm's management can show that they are able to produce goods or services that are considered to be of importance to the state. This might be in providing incomes to single-industry towns, or because a firm enhances Russia's national security or international prestige.

Sectors A and B account for the vast majority of economic activity in Russia. Estimates from a range of different sources, including the IMF and the Russian Federal Antimonopoly Service, suggest that the state-controlled segment of the economy—which includes both the official public sector, SOEs, and enterprises with at least partial state ownership—steadily increased from 2005 to account for as much as 60–70 per cent of Russian GDP by 2015. It is therefore clear that despite having undertaken a series of important market-creating reforms in the 1990s, the Russian state remains the single most important actor in the economy today.

One of the consequences of this outcome is that innovation and productivity growth have suffered. This is because the suppression of competition by the state reduces the incentive for the management of these firms to raise efficiency. Without the threat of competition, the need to restructure and boost productivity is dampened. After all, if the management of an enterprise knows they cannot go bust, why should they bother to change their behaviour?

The relationship between Sectors A and B can be graphically illustrated by looking at the large difference in the sources of demand for the goods and services of Sector A and B. Sector A's natural resources and raw materials account for around 85 per cent of Russia's total merchandise exports in any given year. With the exception of weapons and nuclear power stations, Russia

The reassertion of the state

exports very few manufactured goods. This is why the late US senator John McCain described Russia as 'a gas station masquerading as a country'.

Despite this export profile, Russia is in fact one of the world's top-ten largest manufacturers. This is in stark contrast to many other oil-producing states like Saudi Arabia or Iraq. A wide assortment of manufactured goods is produced in Russia, with the sector estimated to employ around 10 million people in 2015. However, very little of this manufacturing output is sold outside Russia. Instead, it is bought by Russians. This huge gap between the volume of domestic manufacturing production and the comparatively tiny amount sold abroad is explained by the fact that it is the profits made by Sector A, and then redistributed by the state, that support domestic demand for Sector B's output. Without this support, it is unlikely that domestic consumers would buy as many Russian manufactured goods as they currently do.

This system has clearly entrenched the reliance of the economy on strong performance in the oil and gas sector. This is because when oil and gas profits are high, there are more resources to drive up output in Sector B. But when oil and gas profits decline, output in Sector B is dragged down with them. This very simple observation helps explain how and why the fortunes of the Russian economy are so dependent on the performance of the oil and gas sectors.

These two sectors, however, miss an important part of the picture. The market reforms of the 1990s created a significant privately owned part of the economy, or a Sector C. It exists largely outside the state-controlled part of the economy and encompasses many construction and retail groups, business services, and small and medium-sized enterprises (SMEs) across all parts of the economy. These SMEs commonly operate in retail, transportation, business services, and in some of the more knowledge-intensive information and communication technologies.

Firms from within this sector do not generate as much tax as Sector A firms, but nor do they require state support to survive, as in Sector B. Instead, firms from within Sector C are subject to hard budget constraints, which means that their survival depends on their profitability rather than their political contacts. The state does not interfere with economic activity in this sector as much as it does elsewhere. As a result, competition is higher, with correspondingly higher rate of innovation and productivity growth than in Sectors A and B.

Severe obstacles restricted the growth of this sector. One in particular is the weakness of property rights, which often manifests itself in the form of *reiderstvo*, or criminal corporate raiding. This refers to the practice of state officials using a combination of legal and illegal methods to seize businesses or other assets from their owners.

In the 1990s, *reiderstvo* tended to be carried out by private (i.e. non-state) individuals who used corrupt state officials to facilitate their attacks. This changed after 2000 as the state became more powerful. State officials soon became the initiators and beneficiaries of these seizures. While high-profile examples, such as the Yukos affair, tend to dominate the international headlines, a much greater number of attacks have been reported on thousands of smaller enterprises across Russia. This has probably deterred many people from investing in new businesses. Perhaps as a result, only around 20 per cent of the labour force works in SMEs in Russia, compared with a European average of 40 per cent.

The role that the state plays in Russia's system of political economy is of crucial importance. Understanding its role helps to explain both the reasons for much of the inefficiency in the Russian economy, and also the motives that drive the authorities to manipulate and often distort the market. The centralization of state authority that took place under Putin after 2000 significantly expanded the economic functions that it is required to perform. As a result, the state, not the market, emerged as the dominant mechanism for allocating resources in Russia at some point in the early 2000s. This is done by the state employing a range of instruments to coordinate economic activity in Sectors A and B, while also indirectly suppressing the emergence of a dynamic and genuinely competitive Sector C.

It is important to note that no matter which label is used to describe the Russian economy—'state capitalism', 'managed market', or 'hybrid market'—it is very much a system. In this sense, it comprises a number of important interlocking socio-economic groups. While the tendency to focus on the importance of individual leaders like Putin is perhaps natural, the role of the leader in this system is often one of balancing competing interests rather than commanding the economy and a relatively passive population in a more active fashion. This means that while the political system that crystallized under Putin is undoubtedly authoritarian in nature, with correspondingly high levels of corruption and inequality, the leadership has always recognized the importance of sharing resources between politically important groups within society.

Rising prosperity and order

The system of political economy that emerged during Putin's first two terms as president saw the state become stronger than at any point since the disintegration of the Soviet Union. Although this dampened dynamism within the economy, it was not always a bad thing as the state performed a number of important social and political functions. This was made much easier by an average annual rate of economic growth of over 7 per cent (Table 3). One of these was the restoration of a degree of order. Law and order had broken down so much that by the time Putin came to power the murder rate had risen to 28.2 per 100,000 people. This put Russia among the likes of Columbia and Mexico as the

Table 3. Key indicators of economic performance, 2000–8

	2000	2001	2002	2003	2004	2005	2006	2007	2008
GDP, %-change	10.0	5.1	4.7	7.3	7.2	6.4	8.2	8.5	5.2
GDP, USD billion	259	306	345	430	591	763	992	1301	1659
Industrial production, %-change y-o-y	8.7	2.9	3.1	8.9	8.0	5.1	6.3	6.8	0.6
Fixed investments, %-change y-o-y	17.4	11.7	2.9	12.7	16.8	10.2	17.8	23.8	9.5
Retail sales, %-change y-o-y	9.0	11.0	9.3	8.8	13.3	12.8	14.1	16.1	13.7
Exports, USD billion	99.2	96.6	102.1	129.1	177.9	240.0	297.5	346.5	466.3
Imports, USD billion	42.1	51.3	58.4	73.2	94.2	123.8	163.2	223.1	288.7
Unemployment, %	10.6	9.0	7.9	8.2	7.8	7.1	7.1	6.0	6.2
Inflation, %, y-o-y	20.0	21.5	15.8	13.7	10.9	12.7	9.7	9.0	14.1
Federal government balance, % of GDP	2.4	3.0	1.4	1.7	4.3	7.5	7.4	5.4	4.1
Central government debt, % of GDP	52.1	39.2	35.9	28.8	21.3	13.2	8.3	6.7	5.3
External debt, % of GDP	44.5	33.3	29.6	23.7	16.8	9.2	4.4	2.8	1.7
External debt, USD billion	115.5	102.0	102.0	102.0	99.1	69.9	43.2	35.8	28.1

Source: Bank of Finland Institute for Economies in Transition (from official Russian sources).

worst-performing middle-income countries in the world. Under Putin, this declined from 2002 onwards, reaching 16.7 per 100,000 people in 2008. Another important indicator of socio-economic development is life expectancy. This also improved considerably under Putin after falling over the 1990s. In 1994, life expectancy for men was 57 years, 71 years for women, and just 64 years overall. These were the worst figures registered in Russia since the late 1950s. Fortunately, life expectancy began to rise in 2003 and surpassed 1990 levels in 2011. Finally, unemployment, which peaked at over 13 per cent in 1998, dropped to 6 per cent in 2007. Although the state's growing influence was not ideal for economic efficiency, it ensured that important elements of citizens' everyday lives improved in the first decade of the millennium.

As Russia approached the end of Putin's second term as president in the spring of 2008, it was clear that much progress had been made in achieving the goals set out in the millennium manifesto. The power of the Russian state had been restored. It regained control of the 'commanding heights' of the economy, while leaving other, consumer-oriented sectors of the economy to the market. Investment was rising and confidence appeared to have been restored. This economic system proved effective in restoring order and boosting living standards after the chaos and uncertainty of the late 1980s and 1990s.

However, the system created under Putin concealed a number of serious deficiencies in the Russian economy. A new tier of super-wealthy individuals replaced the so-called oligarchs, this time in the form of managers of vast state enterprises like Gazprom and Rosneft. As the shadow of the state grew larger, the space for the development of more dynamic sectors of the economy, such as SMEs in the services and knowledge-based sectors of the economy, grew smaller. Property rights, the foundation of long-term economic prosperity, remained weak. While Putin had largely succeeded in stopping people from killing each other, he failed to stop them from stealing from each other.

State officials were particularly guilty in this respect. Finally, the country remained excessively dependent on the sale of oil and gas to drive economic activity. This problem revealed itself in spectacular fashion just after Putin handed the presidency over to Dmitry Medvedev, a young ally and former manager of Gazprom, in May 2008.

Chapter 5
From modernization to isolation

Russia's new president, Dmitry Medvedev, entered the Kremlin in May 2008 with an ambitious agenda to modernize the Russian economy. This, of course, was nothing new. Leaders throughout Russian history have tried, and sometimes even partially succeeded, in bringing Russia's economy closer in terms of income level and production structure to the world's leading powers. Usually, these leaders had, like Putin before him, used the state as the main vehicle to promote economic development.

But Medvedev sounded different. He showed an interest in the latest technology and spoke of the need to develop the 'Four Is'—infrastructure, investment, institutions, and innovation. Medvedev's goals were outlined in a 4,000-word article titled 'Go Russia!' If successfully achieved, his objectives were designed to harness the latest technologies so that Russia would be a leading power in the 21st-century global economy. He focused on a range of industries, including nuclear power, biotechnology, space technology, and energy efficiency. Medvedev was making all the right noises about the need to modernize and diversify the economy, reduce its dependence on natural resources, and help Russian firms become competitive in knowledge-based industries.

However, Medvedev faced two immediate challenges to the implementation of his plans. First, after enjoying high oil prices in

his early months in office, the economic picture worsened
suddenly when a global financial crisis struck in September.
This pulled down oil prices and drove Russia into a deep recession.
Economic policy was more concerned with combating recession
than it was with building a new economy. Second, and perhaps
more crucially, Medvedev wasn't really in charge. Mr Putin left the
presidency and took up residence across the Moskva river as the
country's prime minister. Formally, Russia's constitution gives
considerably more power to the president than the prime minister.
But this didn't matter. Putin had assembled so much informal
power that most people in the country still saw him as the real
leader. In practical terms, Putin's preference for state-led solutions
to economic policy would continue to prevail regardless of
Medvedev's relatively liberal rhetoric.

The 2008 global financial crisis hit Russia harder than all the
other G20 economies. Global oil prices collapsed and foreign
capital quickly left Russia, pushing the value of the rouble down.
The central bank spent around $200 billion in an effort to control
the devaluation of the currency, while the government embarked
on a massive fiscal expansion—one of the largest in the world as a
proportion of GDP—to support the population, especially those
located in Sector B, where citizens depended on the state for their
incomes. The savings accumulated during the period of oil
surpluses proved vital. Unlike the 1998 financial crisis, the state
was able to redistribute large sums of money to protect the
economy. Nevertheless, the economy shrank by nearly 8 per cent
in 2009, although it returned to growth much faster than many of
its neighbours. Growth of around 4.5 per cent in 2010 and 2011
was considerably faster than both Russia's richer European
neighbours and most other large middle-income countries, such
as Brazil and Turkey, during the same period.

In contrast to 1998, the financial crisis and accompanying
recession did not result in any sharp change in Russia's system of
political economy. Instead, the same methods were employed to

guide the economy through troubled waters. This was further helped by the fact that global oil prices, which dropped to $50 per barrel in March 2009, quickly rose back to over $100 per barrel by the end of 2010. The economic system had proven resilient. Nevertheless, the Russian experience of the Great Recession stimulated the elite into publicly acknowledging the need for economic modernization and diversification. However, they were divided over how best to achieve these objectives: through the state-led initiatives favoured by Putin, or through an intensification of market reform as proposed both by the prime minister and several other influential members of the government?

State-led modernization with a fresh face

Given that real power and authority continued to reside in Putin, it was perhaps no surprise that the next few years saw the continuation of many of the tendencies observed during Putin's two terms as president. The share of the state in total output in key industries—energy, defence-industrial production, finance, and agriculture—continued to grow. A new well-funded state corporation—Rosnano—was created to boost Russia's share of the emerging global nanotechnology market. Headed by Anatoly Chubais, who had previously been in charge of privatization and then of reforming Russia's vast electricity sector, Rosnano embodied much of the government's approach to economic policy at the time. Ambitious targets were touted by slick officials speaking the language of modernization. But, in practice, the methods employed were largely unchanged and the state continued to overshadow the market.

Indeed, in another echo of traditional Russian approaches to economic modernization, the government embarked on an ambitious programme of military modernization that involved a sharp rise in defence spending (Figure 4). This splurge was presented by Putin as a means of supporting a 'locomotive of

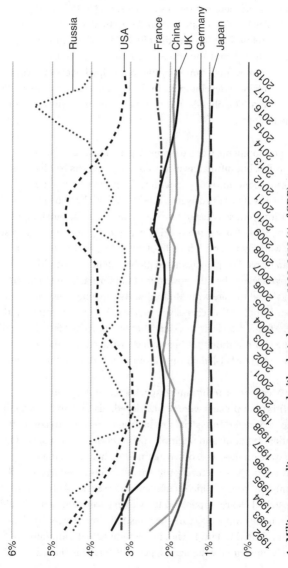

4. Military expenditure compared with selected powers, 1992–2018 (% of GDP).

Russia
USA
France
China
UK
Germany
Japan

6%
5%
4%
3%
2%
1%
0%

1992 1993 1994 1995 1996 1997 1998 1999 2000 2001 2002 2003 2004 2005 2006 2007 2008 2009 2010 2011 2012 2013 2014 2015 2016 2017 2018

75

technological development'. Critics, including some within the government, argued that the resources allocated to building nuclear missiles, fighter aircraft, and warships would be better employed rebuilding Russia's dilapidated infrastructure or in improving health and education. Others pointed out that spending money on the military had not helped boost innovation and technological development in the civilian economy during the Soviet period. The liberal-minded finance minister, Alexei Kudrin, resigned in protest.

These developments were, to some degree, masked by some high-profile, but ultimately inconsequential, efforts by Medvedev to present economic policy in a more favourable light. One example was Russia's answer to Silicon Valley: the Skolkovo Innovation Centre. Located in a leafy suburb on the outskirts of Moscow, Skolkovo was intended to bring in the best and brightest minds working in key high-technology industries to work with Russian firms. The plan attracted global attention. Arnold Schwarzenegger, then the governor of California, home to Silicon Valley, visited the site with Medvedev. Before long, however, familiar complaints of excessive bureaucracy and corruption were heard. After a decade, it was clear that Skolkovo had failed to ignite the type of innovation that Medvedev envisaged, whether of the 'bottom-up', market-led nature, or of the 'top-down', state-led type.

While Medvedev's ambitions to spark a technology-led modernization process were not achieved, his time in the Kremlin was not a disaster. Industrial production rose and the economy expanded. Inflation and unemployment, both of which spiked in 2009, were on their way down again. But Russia's leaders were well aware of the structural problems that continued to afflict the economy. Oil prices, which remained above $100 per barrel over 2011–12, had clearly supported Russia's recovery. But what would happen if they dipped again? Responsibility for answering this question shifted to Putin, who, in September 2011, announced that he would run for the presidency in 2012. This caused disappointment among some in Russia's elite and urban classes who had hoped that Medvedev would be given the chance to make better progress with his own modernization agenda. For several months at the end of 2011 and in early 2012, Moscow staged large protests against Putin's return to the presidency.

Technocrats, state managers, and the 'siloviki'

Medvedev's apparent struggle to implement any meaningful measures to ignite the growth of new industries highlighted the struggle between three broad groups to dominate economic policy in Russia. Although these groups do not include everybody who seeks to shape economic policy, they do capture the salient contours of the policy environment.

The first group—what is often labelled the 'economic bloc'— comprised well-educated technocrats, like Alexei Kudrin and Elvira Nabiullina, who occupied leading positions in the Ministry of Finance, the central bank, and the Ministry for Economic Development. These individuals tended to extol the virtues of sound macroeconomic policy—primarily the avoidance of budget deficits and a commitment to low inflation—and expressed support for market-augmenting reforms, such as strengthening the rule of law and reducing support for inefficient enterprises.

The second group—which can be described as the 'state managers'—was made up of the officials in charge of Russia's vast state corporations and state-owned enterprises. This group tended to be dominated by career bureaucrats or individuals with historically close links to Vladimir Putin. Examples range from German Gref, the head of Sberbank, Russia's largest bank; Anatoly Chubais, as mentioned above, the former architect of privatization and later the head of the state corporation Rosnano; and Sergei Chemezov, head of Rostec, a vast empire of manufacturing enterprises, many of which are involved in military production. State managers tended to be less concerned with macroeconomic objectives and more focused on expanding their own firms, often lobbying the government for additional resources or for tax breaks.

The third group—the so-called *siloviki*, roughly translated as 'power people'—refer to personnel drawn from Russia's armed forces and uniformed services (*silovye struktury*). After Putin was elected president in 2000, many observers drew attention to the apparent increase in the appointment of *siloviki* to key positions in Russia's political system and economy. Using sensationalist language, *The Economist* described this process as the creation of a 'neo-KGB state'. While many of these descriptions proved to be exaggerated, it is certainly the case that some powerful *siloviki* occupy important positions in Russia's political economy. The most obvious example is Igor Sechin, an ex-KGB officer and head of Rosneft, the country's largest oil company, making him both a *silovik* and a state manager. Many analysts considered Sechin to be the second most powerful person in Russia. The influence of the *siloviki* can also be observed in the formulation of policy towards foreign investment and information security.

In practice, no single group dominated economic policy entirely. Instead, each was able to shape specific areas of public policy. The technocrats, for example, tended to prevail in matters of fiscal and monetary policy. With the exception of periods of recession, Russia recorded budget surpluses. Public debt was very low and inflation declined in most years. But state managers were often successful in expanding their sprawling conglomerates by lobbying for resources from the state. The *siloviki*, in their turn, succeeded in ensuring that security concerns shaped economic policies, especially in restricting foreign investment in areas defined by them to be of strategic importance.

Putin's return to the Kremlin

Putin's inauguration took place in the Kremlin on 7 May 2012, with Medvedev replacing Putin as prime minister. Putin had already laid out his agenda for the economy during his election campaign. Echoing many of the same themes addressed in his millennium manifesto, Putin penned an article in one of Russia's leading business newspapers, *Vedomosti*, in January entitled 'We need a new economy'. He restated his commitment to economic modernization and proposed a series of ambitious goals, dubbed the 'May Decrees'. It became official government policy to reach these goals, which included creating millions of jobs in high-tech industry, improving living standards, developing Russia's Far East, and implementing a programme of rapid military modernization. However, critics questioned whether these ambitions could be met if Putin refused to change the economic system built during his first two terms as president.

These expressions of doubt seemed to be justified. In 2012, the rate of growth slowed to 3.7 per cent, and then even further to 1.3 per cent in 2013. This was significantly lower than the 1999–2008 average of over 7 per cent. Investment fell slightly in 2013 as major investment projects associated with the Sochi Olympics, as well as some major energy infrastructure projects, were completed. The share of investment in GDP, which had been a perennial problem in Russia, remained low at around 22 per cent (Figure 5). According to most assessments, the share of investment needed to be closer to 30 per cent if Russia was to experience modernization. This is because investment results in the installation of new, more productive, machinery and infrastructure that makes a higher rate of growth possible. The slowdown in the first two years of Putin's third term as president took place despite oil prices remaining at historically high levels.

War in Ukraine and sanctions

In 2014, Russia's foreign policy took a sharp turn that led to conflict with neighbouring Ukraine and, as a result, confrontation with the United States, the European Union (EU), and their allies. Russia annexed Crimea and then became involved in a military

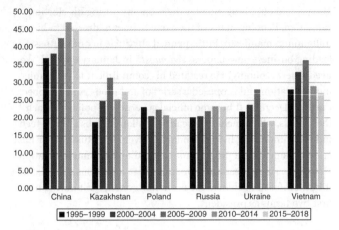

5. Gross fixed capital formation (investment) in Russia and selected populous post-communist economies (% of GDP, five-year averages, 1995–2018).

conflict in the south-east of Ukraine. The geopolitical roots of this conflict are complex, but one of the most important outcomes for the Russian economy was that the Western alliance and Ukraine imposed a range of economic sanctions on Russia over the course of the summer of 2014. Initially, the United States and the EU coordinated sanctions policy together. However, from 2017 onwards the United States imposed additional sanctions without the support of its EU allies.

In the immediate aftermath of the annexation of Crimea, individuals within Russia's elite were targeted with asset freezes and travel bans. Later in the summer, after the MH17 airliner was shot down over eastern Ukraine, so-called sectoral sanctions were imposed. These targeted firms in Russia's defence, energy, and finance sectors. In economic terms, the most important sanctions included restrictions on loans to these sectors; the prohibition of Western involvement in new energy projects; and a ban on arms sales to and from Russia. In response, Moscow imposed so-called 'counter sanctions' on Western food imports.

In simple terms, sanctions can be described as economic instruments used by 'sender' states to impose economic pain on 'target' states to achieve political objectives. In practice, however, sanctions are often enacted without there being any serious expectation on the part of the sender state(s) that the target state might alter its behaviour. This was certainly true in relation to Russia's annexation of Crimea. Very few observers or officials seriously expected that sanctions would result in Crimea being 'returned' to Ukraine. But there was at least some expectation that Western economic pressure might either cause the Russian leadership to reduce the support given to separatists in eastern Ukraine, or, at the very least, deter it from expanding the conflict even further. As well as seeking to shape Russian policy in Ukraine, Western sanctions were designed to send a clear signal to other states in the international community that similar actions to those undertaken by Russia would incur a significant cost.

Another collapse in oil prices

Western sanctions were quickly followed by a collapse in global oil prices. The average price of crude oil had hovered around $110 per barrel from 2011 to the summer of 2014. But prices plummeted over the winter, dropping to $47 per barrel in January 2015. This was caused by slowing growth in Europe and Asia's largest economies, and by the rapid expansion of oil supplies in North America. This caused a sharp depreciation of the rouble, which lost around 50 per cent of its dollar value between January 2013 and January 2015. Russia, it seemed, was yet again suffering for its overdependence on oil and gas. The economy, which had been slowing down since Putin returned to the Kremlin in early 2012, was now buffeted by geopolitical and economic shocks. Like Medvedev's modernization agenda that was derailed by the global financial crisis of 2008–9, Putin's programme of executing the 'May Decrees' was now sidelined by the need to respond to sanctions and the fall in oil prices.

The dual shock of sanctions and the collapse in oil prices triggered a protracted recession that began in early 2015 and stretched into 2016 (Table 4). GDP fell by nearly 3 per cent during this period. Investment, which had begun to fall even before the summer of 2014, shrank by over 11 per cent. Unemployment rose, albeit modestly. However, underemployment—where people were officially employed but were not working full hours—rose faster. The depreciation of the rouble caused inflation to rise from under 7 per cent in 2013 to over 15 per cent in 2015. Living standards began to fall significantly for the first time since Putin came to power in 1999. The federal budget, which had recorded surpluses for most years since 1999, fell into deficit again. Although the economy returned to growth in 2017, it grew by a mere 1.5 per cent followed by growth of 2.3 per cent in 2018. This was significantly slower than the rate of global growth, which was closer to 4 per cent. With living standards being squeezed and Russia's share in the global economy shrinking, modernization and diversification appeared further away than ever.

Russia's response to sanctions

Economic policy was soon dominated by the leadership's attempts to deal with the negative effects of Western sanctions. They devised policies to reduce the impact of Western sanctions and to cushion Russia from similar measures in the future. In broad terms, the Russian response, which was applied in all three of the sectors targeted by the USA and its allies, was focused on enhancing Russia's economic sovereignty. They hoped to achieve this through state-directed efforts to boost Russia's domestic economic capabilities. Replacing Western goods and services with domestically produced equivalents was labelled 'import substitution'. Where this proved challenging, Russian firms also

Table 4. Key indicators of economic performance, 2009–18

	2009	2010	2011	2012	2013	2014	2015	2016	2017	2018
GDP, %-change	-7.8	4.5	4.3	3.7	1.8	0.7	-2.3	0.3	1.6	2.3
GDP, USD billion	1221	1524	2050	2193	2292	2048	1355	1287	1579	1650
Industrial production, %-change y-o-y	-10.7	7.3	5.0	3.4	0.4	2.5	-0.8	2.2	2.1	2.9
Fixed investments, %-change y-o-y	-13.5	6.3	10.8	6.8	0.8	-1.5	-10.1	-0.2	4.8	4.3
Retail sales, %-change y-o-y	-5.1	6.5	7.1	6.3	3.9	2.7	-10.0	-4.8	1.3	2.8
Exports, USD billion	297.2	392.7	515.4	527.4	521.8	496.8	341.4	281.7	353.1	443.1
Imports, USD billion	183.9	245.6	318.6	335.8	341.3	307.9	193.0	191.5	238.4	248.7
Unemployment, %	8.3	7.3	6.5	5.5	5.5	5.2	5.6	5.5	5.2	4.8
Inflation, %, y-o-y	11.7	6.8	8.4	5.1	6.8	7.8	15.5	7.0	3.7	2.9
Federal government balance, % of GDP	-6.0	-3.9	0.7	-0.1	-0.4	-0.4	-2.4	-3.4	-1.4	2.6
Central government debt, % of GDP	7.8	8.5	8.6	9.7	10.5	11.2	11.0	12.3	12.9	11.5
External debt, % of GDP	2.4	2.1	1.6	2.4	2.7	2.0	2.2	3.0	3.5	2.7
External debt, USD billion	29.5	32.2	33.6	53.5	61.0	41.0	30.0	38.9	55.4	43.8

Source: Bank of Finland Institute for Economies in Transition (from official Russian sources).

sourced banned goods and services from new economic partners, primarily located in Asia.

In the energy industry, a determined effort to invest resources in the production of oil and gas equipment took place. Imports of oil and gas equipment from non-Western countries rose, reducing Russia's previous dependence on the West for technology. This was accompanied by an increase in the use of non-Western sources of capital, with China leading the way by investing in several large-scale oil and gas projects. During this time, Russia signed new agreements to supply energy to China, India, and other rapidly growing Asian economies.

Similar efforts were made in the defence industry. Here, policymakers implemented an ambitious programme to replace banned components and weapons systems with domestically produced analogues, including helicopter and ship engines. This was accompanied by efforts to strengthen defence-industrial cooperation with several non-Western states, such as China and India.

Adaptive measures formulated by policymakers in the financial system also created the conditions for a more self-reliant financial system. These included the creation of a new national payments system, as well as cards to replace Visa and Mastercard. The central bank conducted a vigorous attempt to clean up the banking system by withdrawing banking licences from poorly performing banks. Russian firms also sought to access loans from non-Western countries, although this achieved only modest success. These measures were intended by policymakers to reduce the susceptibility of Russia's financial system to any potential escalation of sanctions in the future.

Russia's 'counter sanctions' achieved mixed results. They boosted domestic food production, which grew even as the wider economy entered recession in 2015–16. Agricultural output grew by around

5 per cent between 2014 and 2016. Russia also registered post-Soviet records for grain harvests and exports. However, this came at the expense of higher prices for Russian consumers, especially in the first months of the policy's implementation. New sources of food from the likes of China, Chile, and Brazil began to replace Western food products.

Military modernization

Meanwhile, as Russia's leaders came to grips with sanctions, the programme for military modernization approved in 2011 continued to be rolled out. The geopolitical tensions that followed the conflict in Ukraine caused rearmament to be one of the government's top priorities. As the rearmament process gathered momentum, total Russian military expenditure grew from 3.8 per cent of GDP in 2010 to nearly 5.5 per cent in 2015 (Figure 4). This amount was well in excess of the NATO average (1.5 per cent of GDP) and that of the USA (3.3 per cent) and China (1.9 per cent). The amount allocated to the procurement of new equipment grew from 1 per cent of GDP in 2010 to nearly 2.5 per cent of GDP in 2015. However, Russia's armed forces had been starved of funding over the 1990s and were in desperate need of new equipment (Figure 6).

This expansion of military spending caused a shift in the composition of federal government spending. In 2010, military expenditure accounted for just over 15 per cent of total federal government spending. By 2015 its share had risen to well over 25 per cent. This came at the expense of federal spending on health and education, which saw their shares of spending decline. Yet the share of social welfare spending, which includes pensions payments, did not decline, again demonstrating the government's determination to avoid angering a large and sometimes vocal segment of the population. As military modernization progressed, the government began to shift federal spending back towards other areas of social spending. Defence spending peaked in 2016 and then declined as a share of GDP afterwards. Budget

6. Military modernization.

projections into the early 2020s indicated that the share of defence spending would decline towards the historic average.

The 'Kalashnikov' economy

The response to sanctions and the ongoing commitment to maintaining a strong and capable military meant that Russia was more secure and better equipped to deal with geopolitical competition. While Western sanctions caused some initial disruption—especially at the end of 2014 and in early 2015—the impact on targeted sectors subsided after a relatively short period of time. There was no noticeably negative impact on oil and gas production. Instead, oil and gas production rose. In the defence industry, sanctions delayed the Ministry of Defence's plans for naval rearmament, but most other areas of defence-industrial production proceeded largely to plan. The financial sector also experienced substantial disruption in the winter of 2014–15. However, the measures taken by policymakers created the conditions for a more self-reliant and secure financial system.

The relative success in cushioning Russia from the impact of sanctions was achievable largely because of the active role played by the state in Russia's system of political economy. Although many considered this to be a cause of weakness before 2014, it proved to be a source of durability under conditions of economic warfare. However, in 'sanctions proofing' the economy, and by diverting scarce resources to defence, policymakers had imposed important constraints that were likely to shackle the economy for years to come. In particular, the Russian policy response emphasized yet more state-led measures which further weakened the development of the market. The model of political economy built under Putin became more entrenched, not less. Security, it appeared, carried a heavy price.

Although the rate of growth after 2013 was relatively low, and certainly lower than Russia's leaders would have liked, the successes of the emphasis on stability should not be underestimated. Aided by prudent macroeconomic policy over the past two decades, Russia has tended to register a 'triple surplus'. This means that it runs a surplus on its current account (i.e. aggregate savings exceed aggregate investment), a trade surplus, and a federal budget surplus. Russia's sovereign debt-to-GDP ratio of around 11 per cent in 2018 was the lowest of all the G20 economies. Regular triple surpluses allowed the authorities to build up a substantial hoard of savings. For example, foreign exchange reserves exceeded $500 billion in the middle of 2019.

The indicators that arguably matter most to the general population—unemployment and inflation—remained comparatively healthy. Because the labour force shrank after 2010 due to demographic changes, unemployment hovered at post-Soviet low levels of around 5 per cent for nearly a decade. Russia's problem as far as the labour market was concerned was the shortage of skilled and unskilled workers, not large-scale unemployment. Inflation also remained near post-Soviet lows as Russia entered 2020.

Nevertheless, President Putin repeatedly expressed the belief that economic policy should provide both greater security and economic modernization. But Putin's preferred policy course that delivered macroeconomic stability and financial security failed to stimulate dynamic growth. The economists Clifford Gaddy and Barry Ickes described this as a 'Kalashnikov economy'—that is, a system that is durable in political terms yet unsophisticated when measured by economic efficiency. Nevertheless, if Russia's rate of growth consistently lags behind the global rate of growth, its security and prosperity may suffer over the long run. After all, slow growth will result in a relatively smaller economy and a comparatively poorer population, which would undermine Russia's place as one of the world's 'great powers'.

Another state-led initiative for economic development

New measures to address Russia's impending relative economic decline were revealed by Vladimir Putin after his fourth inauguration as president in May 2018. Putin outlined a six-year programme that envisaged a federal government spending surge on thirteen 'national projects'. The national projects were designed to help achieve nine strategic objectives, including raising the annual rate of economic growth to above the global average, reducing poverty levels by half, increasing population growth, and raising living standards. These objectives were again dubbed the 'May Decrees', and in effect replaced those issued in 2012. One of these goals was to make Russia the fifth largest economy in the world at purchasing power parity (PPP) by 2024. Many analysts use PPP rather than market exchange rates to estimate the value of economic activity in a country because it accounts for differences in relative costs. Non-traded goods and services tend to be cheaper in lower-income countries, like Russia. For example, the price of an Uber ride of the same distance is significantly higher in London than in Moscow. This is because wages tend to be lower in poorer countries, and services such as Uber are relatively labour intensive. Using PPP to measure GDP results in Russia accounting for a larger share of global GDP.

Putin's new economic policy agenda did not, however, represent a shift away from the conservative fiscal and monetary policies that characterized economic policy earlier under his rule. Instead, extra expenditure was financed by increasing the value-added tax rate from 18 per cent to 20 per cent, raising taxes on oil and gas extraction, reducing support to oil refiners, and increasing the retirement age. As a result, any additional expenditure was funded through corresponding tax rises elsewhere. The accompanying budget detailed a shift in government spending away from security and social welfare towards greater support for infrastructure projects and spending on health and education. Putin and his government, it appeared, were wary of neglecting the needs of the people to pay for security for too much longer.

While the latest development strategy is likely to serve as the focal point of economic policy for the foreseeable future, it remains the case that it is, in essence, not very different from other development plans proposed by Putin in the past. It aims to stimulate a faster rate of economic growth but without altering the fundamental institutional structure, for example, by improving property rights and strengthening the rule of law. After nearly twenty years as the leader of Russia, Putin was clearly reluctant to weaken the state's grip over the economy to promote economic development.

Chapter 6
Russia in the global economy

A foreign visitor to a large city in Russia today is likely to encounter many of the trappings of the global economy that can be seen in other globally connected cities across the world. Next to the onion domes of Russia's Orthodox churches, they will find neon signs advertising the latest Chinese or Korean mobile phones, financial services provided by familiar US banks, and roads clogged with Japanese SUVs and luxury German cars. Restaurants serving every conceivable cuisine from across the world provide wines from as far as Argentina and New Zealand, and serve produce sourced from as far away as Australia and Brazil.

Russia's presence in the global economy is also hard to miss. Whether it be Gazprom sponsoring Champions League football matches, mining companies uncovering diamonds and other precious stones and metals in Africa, or Turkish beaches heaving with Russian tourists, Russia's imprint on the global economy is much greater and more visible than it has ever been. In many ways, Russia today appears very much to be a 21st-century economy: open, networked, and digital. In this respect, the contrast with the Soviet Union could not be greater.

Much has changed. Yet for all the considerable and impressive transformation that took place after the end of the Cold War, other aspects of Russia's role in the global economy have proven more resistant to change. Nearly thirty years after the disintegration of the Soviet Union, Russia continues to export largely the same types of goods as it did in the 1980s: principally natural resources and armaments. Perhaps just as importantly, many of these exports are controlled by groups owned by, or close to, the Russian state. And while Moscow, St Petersburg, and other large regional cities are important nodes within the wider network of global flows of goods, services, capital, and people, large swathes of Russia remain largely disconnected from the outside world.

Perhaps most importantly, Russia's economic fortunes today are, for better or for worse, heavily shaped by events in the wider global economy. As a country that is relatively open to trade, and which provides a large proportion of the world's hydrocarbons, natural resources, and food, what happens in Russia is of considerable importance to the global economy. For Russia, the reverse is also true. All of Russia's recent recessions have been caused by a downturn in global commodity markets. And its periods of fastest growth have come when the wider world economy was in good health. Managing this sensitivity to the global economy has become one of the key challenges facing Russian policymakers today.

Russia's reintegration with the global economy

After the collapse of the Soviet Union at the end of 1991, Russia embarked on a process of reintegration with the global economy in a rapid and broad-based fashion. Russia quickly opened up its domestic market. Rules prohibiting trade and investment with and from foreign firms were removed at the stroke of a pen. This led to a sharp rise in imports of consumer goods, machinery, and technology, as well as capital, from its former capitalist adversaries in the West. As time went on, trade with China and the wider Asian economy also grew quickly.

However, Russia's new leaders were faced with forging a path of reintegration whilst simultaneously dealing with the collapse of the Soviet empire. This process of disintegration took two forms. First, the ex-socialist members of the CMEA in central and eastern Europe were, by the early 1990s, hurtling at full speed towards closer integration with western Europe. As this process unfolded, trade ties between Russia and its former Warsaw Pact allies shrank sharply. Second, and for Russia even more importantly, economic relations with the fourteen other former republics of the USSR were now a matter of foreign economic policy. Without orders from central planners in Moscow, the dense trade linkages between enterprises spread across the newly independent republics began to disappear. This made an important contribution to the savage recession that gripped the countries of the region in the 1990s. It also resulted in a reorientation in the direction of economic relations for all ex-Soviet republics. The Baltic states quickly gravitated towards Scandinavia and northern Europe, while the central Asian states shifted towards trading more with China and other states to their south.

The reformers in charge of economic policy in Russia saw reintegration with the global economy as serving both political and economic purposes. In economic terms, the liberalization of foreign trade and investment was intended to solve two of the most important flaws of the centrally planned economic system: the distorted price structure, resulting from the previous system of state-administered prices; and the centralized and highly integrated production system formed by large monopolistic enterprises. Reformers hoped that by opening Russia up to more trade they would 'import' world prices and 'inject' more competition into the domestic economy that was still dominated by a small number of very large domestic producers that had previously been supported by the state.

It was also envisaged that foreign direct investment (FDI) from multinational companies (MNCs) would expose Russian enterprises to much greater competition. It was hoped they would bring technological and organizational 'spillovers' to the rest of the economy. Reformers also hoped that access to global capital markets would allow domestic firms with limited access to domestic sources of savings (due to the underdevelopment of the Russian financial system) to borrow the funds required for investment projects.

Just as importantly, the economic effects of closer integration with the global economy were not intended by reformers to be politically neutral. 'Importing' prices and 'injecting' competition would threaten the pre-existing network of relations between Soviet-era officials and industrial managers by exposing Russian enterprises to foreign competition and subjecting them to the imposition of 'hard budget constraints'. In simple terms, competition from abroad was intended to force domestic businesses to become more modern, efficient, and competitive. As a result, it was hoped that integration with the global economy would also contribute towards political reform by undermining the power of entrenched officials and businesses that had dominated the Soviet economy. These efforts towards greater integration with the global economy were therefore viewed as an important part of a much wider struggle to create a healthy market economy and a more democratic polity.

In practice, the ambitions of reformers were only partially realized. The liberalization of the domestic economy and of foreign trade in early 1992 led to the rapid emergence of a flourishing retail sector. Street markets and kiosks emerged across Russia. A wide range of imported goods now filled the previously empty shelves of retail stores, although at this stage only a few fortunate people were in a position to afford them. However, the injection of external competition proved insufficient to force all Soviet-era enterprises to restructure. Instead, those that were large or politically important lobbied state authorities for support to help them survive the onslaught of competition from abroad.

This prevented the emergence of a globally competitive manufacturing sector from the ruins of Soviet industry. The only industrial firms that were able to withstand foreign competition without state support were those located in the natural resources sector and some of the more efficient firms from the Soviet defence industry. The latter included some advanced arms manufacturers and the complex of enterprises that worked in the nuclear power industry.

Hopes for a surge in foreign investment were also dashed. The economic and political turbulence of the 1990s, along with the paucity of lucrative investment opportunities, meant that inflows of FDI were relatively modest. Where they did take place, they were largely restricted to the natural resources sector and some areas of retail in Russia's larger cities. Some large MNCs, such as BP, Shell, and Chevron, were able to take the risks associated with doing business in Russia. But most foreign companies avoided any significant exposure, thus reducing the positive spillovers that reformers hoped would come with foreign investment.

Russia's openness to other forms of capital inflow also failed to achieve the effects envisaged by reformers. After the most traumatic period of the economic depression was over in the mid-1990s, capital inflows to Russia rose sharply. Unfortunately, rather than fuelling a boom in lending to Russian firms seeking to create competitive businesses, portfolio investment tended to be focused on the high returns on offer from funding the government's burgeoning budget deficit or inflating Moscow's nascent but rapidly growing stock exchange. While a few well-placed enterprises benefited from these inflows of foreign capital, the wider Russian economy remained, for the most part, starved of capital. This prevented the modernization of the production base of the Russian economy, preventing enterprises from developing new products and services.

This uneven pattern of integration with the global economy brought disaster in the summer of 1998. In 1997, the Asian financial crisis caused global commodity prices to slump. Within months, the Russian economy began to slow down. This was especially significant because 1997 was the first year that the Russian Federation had posted positive GDP growth. Faced with dwindling export revenues and tax receipts, the Russian government was forced to borrow more to cover its growing budget deficit. In August 1998, the Russian government, which had offered increasingly exorbitant returns on short-term bonds to attract lenders, could no longer afford to keep up with repayments. As a result, the government defaulted on the debt it owed to Russian banks. This caused the collapse of large swathes of the Russian banking system, along with the disappearance of much of the savings of the nascent middle class.

A painful devaluation of the rouble followed and inflation rose sharply again. It seemed as if new depths of economic despair lay ahead for the weary Russian population. The impact was also felt well beyond Russia's borders. Because Russian banks had borrowed from foreign banks to lend to the Russian government, hedge funds and banks across the world suffered enormous losses as their loans to Russian banks went sour. At one point in 1998, this contagion effect looked as though it would cause serious damage to the entire US financial system. Long-Term Capital Management (LTCM), a hedge fund, suffered enormous losses as a result of the Russian default. This raised fears that LTCM would fail and trigger a catastrophic chain reaction in the US financial system. In the end, only a $3.7 billion bailout, organized by the New York Federal Reserve, prevented a wider financial crisis.

By the end of the 1990s, it was clear that Russia was much more closely integrated with the global economy than the Soviet Union had ever been. The country was open to inflows of goods, services, and capital on an unprecedented scale. But with this came increased vulnerability to external shocks. This vulnerability was exacerbated by the country's failure to build a modern and diverse economic structure to complement its natural comparative advantage in the extraction and export of natural resources. Nevertheless, on the eve of the millennium it was clear that, despite the problems encountered during the traumatic 1990s, Russia was emerging as an increasingly important, if somewhat unstable, part of the global economy.

Russia's place in the global economy today

The system of political economy that delivered such positive results in the first decade of the millennium was based on the links with the global economy created in the 1990s. In particular, the unprecedented expansion of the Chinese economy in the new millennium caused a once-in-a-lifetime surge in global demand for raw materials. Prices for oil and other natural resources rose as global supply struggled to keep up with demand. This, along with the foundations laid by the reforms of the 1990s, provided the impetus for the long-awaited return to growth in the Russian economy. Capital inflows returned. Foreign investment in Russia's rapidly growing consumer sector surged. And rapidly rising profits for Russia's natural resources firms—both state and privately owned—turned them into global players with global ambitions. Integration with the world economy seemed, after the uncertain start in the 1990s, to be irreversible. Even the imposition of Western sanctions in 2014 failed to result in 'deglobalization'. What, then, is Russia's place in the global economy today?

Perhaps the most important observation is that, even after three decades of mixed economic fortunes, Russia remains a comparatively large economy. According to IMF data, at $1.6 trillion, the Russian economy was the eleventh largest in the world in dollar terms in 2018, accounting for just 1.8 per cent of global GDP. This is slightly smaller than Italy and Canada, and just a little larger than South Korea and Australia. Expressed in current US dollars, Russia's per capita income was around $11,000, which amounts to around 15 per cent of per capita income in the USA, and just over 30 per cent of the EU average. Put into wider perspective, this is lower than Poland and Chile, but higher than Brazil and Turkey.

However, measured at PPP—that is, adjusted for differences in the cost of living—the picture is strikingly different. GDP in 2018 was over $4 trillion, accounting for around 3.5 per cent of global GDP. According to this measure, Russia was the sixth largest economy in the world, and the second largest in Europe, only slightly behind Germany. Measured at PPP, per capita income was nearly $28,000, half the US level and nearly three-quarters of the EU average. While Russia is not an economic giant like the USA or China, it does belong in the second tier of regional heavyweights like Japan, India, Brazil, and Germany.

Russia is also, in statistical terms, a comparatively open economy. This is usually expressed as the sum of imports and exports as a proportion of a country's GDP. According to World Bank data, trade accounted for 47 per cent of Russia's GDP in 2018. This is more open than many other large low- and middle-income economies such as Brazil (24 per cent), China (38 per cent), and India (41 per cent). Russia, then, is an open economy for a country of its size. It is also relatively open when compared with several large high-income economies, including the USA (28 per cent) and Japan (36 per cent). This openness means that the Russian economy is sensitive to developments well beyond its own borders and, in most instances, over which it has little control.

The composition of Russia's imports and exports, however, reveals that Russia's links with global trade are concentrated in a relatively small number of areas. On the export side, natural resources continue to account for the vast majority of Russia's sales. In this respect, Russia is as dependent on the sale abroad of natural resources as the Soviet Union once was. Hydrocarbons—oil,

oil products, natural gas, and coal—account for most of this, making up anywhere between 55 and 75 per cent of total Russian exports in any one year. Along with the USA and Saudi Arabia, Russia is in the top-three producers of crude oil in the world (the ranking varies by year). As domestic oil consumption has declined slightly in recent years, Russia's exportable surplus of oil is the second largest in the world, behind only Saudi Arabia. This has brought considerable volatility: downturns in global prices in 2008 and 2014 both caused painful recessions.

Other non-hydrocarbon natural resources, such as metals, minerals, and forestry products, account for nearly 10 per cent of total Russian exports in most years. While this is a relatively small share of Russia's exports, the share of Russian mining companies in the global production of a number of precious and strategically important metals and minerals is very high. In 2017, Russia was the world's largest producer of diamonds (around a third of global production), with most extracted by ALROSA, a partially state-owned mining company. Russia is also the third largest producer of gold. In recent years, Russia has become an increasingly important exporter of agricultural products, as shown in 2018 when it became the largest exporter of wheat in the world, slightly ahead of the United States. This was in stark contrast to the Soviet period when it was forced to import wheat from the USA and Canada.

Outside natural resources and agricultural products, Russia is globally competitive in only a few other industries. Since the 1990s, Russia has consistently held the position as the world's second largest exporter (second to the United States) of armaments, and is a world leader in the production and export of machinery for nuclear power stations. In both cases, this is a distinct and enduring legacy of the Soviet Union's investment in, and prioritization of, the defence industry. Only a few new globally competitive industries have emerged since the Soviet era, the most notable of which is the software industry. Compared to the likes of the USA and India, Russia is a medium-sized software exporter, although it is among the fastest growing.

Thus, while Russia is often misleadingly characterized as a mere 'petro state', it is clear that it is an extremely important producer and exporter of some of the world's most sensitive and strategically important goods. For this reason alone, Russia's importance to the global economy should not be underestimated.

Russia's import profile also continues, in many ways, to be similar to that of the Soviet Union. Despite its position as one of the world's ten largest producers of manufactured goods, Russia imports large volumes of high-quality capital goods (machinery, advanced machine tools, etc.) and consumer products. According to UN data, capital goods accounted for the highest proportion of imported goods (nearly a third of all imports in 2017), followed by industrial supplies and consumer goods. These areas where import penetration is highest highlight those areas where Russian industry remains relatively weak. They also represent areas where foreign firms, such as Siemens and Caterpillar, as well as luxury consumer brands, see Russia as an important market.

If the overall structure of Russia's foreign trade exhibits considerable continuity with the Soviet Union, the composition of its trade partners is very different. Although it remains the case that the majority of Russia's trade is conducted with the countries of the European Union (EU)—with the EU accounting for 46 per cent of Russia's exports in 2018, and 38 per cent of Russia's imports—trade ties with non-Western economies have grown sharply. Like so many other countries, the imprint of Asian economies has grown considerably over the past three decades. China is now Russia's single largest partner, accounting for 10 per cent of Russian exports and the source of 22 per cent of imports. Asia more widely—including India, South Korea, Japan, and Vietnam—accounts for around 10 per cent of Russia's exports and nearly 15 per cent of imports. Outside Asia, rapidly growing economic powers like Turkey are increasing in importance, too. In 2018, it was the destination for 5 per cent of Russian exports.

These trends look set to continue. The enormous Power of Siberia (*Sila Sibiri*) gas pipeline to China that is due to be completed in 2020, along with the construction of liquefied natural gas (LNG) terminals in the Arctic, will cause exports to China and Asia more widely to rise significantly over the coming years. Turkey's role as a trade partner looks set to grow, too, when the Turkish Stream gas pipeline system is completed. This is likely to be accompanied by the sale of armaments and nuclear power machinery.

Russia is also an important destination for, and source of, capital flows. In aggregate terms, the country is usually a net saver, running a surplus on the current account of its balance of payments. This occurs when domestic savings exceed domestic investment. These surplus savings are often invested in other countries. As a result, when compared with other middle-income countries, Russia displays a high ratio of outward foreign direct investment (OFDI) to GDP due to large Russian enterprises owning assets abroad. Very often this was the result of Russian energy or metals firms acquiring downstream assets (so-called 'market-seeking' OFDI), or because they acquired foreign technological capabilities and know-how ('technology-seeking' OFDI). Although it is often alleged that the presence of Russian firms abroad is motivated by political objectives, most evidence suggests that they display the same profit-seeking motives as other companies from across the world.

As the economy recovered from the slump of the 1990s, Russia also attracted substantial flows of inward foreign direct investment (IFDI). For much of the decade prior to the imposition of sanctions, Russia's stock of IFDI hovered around the 30 per cent of GDP level. This exceeded many other large low- and middle-income economies, including Brazil, China, India, and Mexico, as well as several high-income economies like

Italy and South Korea. However, a large proportion of this 'foreign' investment is often not foreign at all. Instead, it is capital that originates from Russia but is repatriated via offshore havens like Jersey, the British Virgin Islands, and Cyprus. Nevertheless, many of the world's largest foreign firms are present in Russia's natural resources, retail, manufacturing, and financial services sectors. Yet, unlike countries like China or other post-socialist countries in central and eastern Europe, Russia did not become as closely integrated with global value chains (GVCs).

In addition, foreigners hold shares in many of Russia's most high-profile enterprises, with the likes of Rosneft and Gazprom listed on the London Stock Exchange. Most notably, BP holds nearly a 20 per cent share in Rosneft, with the Russian company accounting for one in every three barrels of oil produced by BP. Other major shareholders in Rosneft include the Qatar Investment Authority and CEFC China Energy.

After spending most of the 1990s and early 2000s consumed with its own domestic economic challenges, Russia became much more active in seeking to shape the governance of the global economy. Russia went from being a recipient of IMF and World Bank support to a member of the World Trade Organization (WTO) in 2012, and a shareholder in the New Development Bank (formerly the BRICS Development Bank) in 2014.

As the domestic economy grew stronger, Russia reinvigorated efforts to strengthen ties between a number of ex-Soviet states through various integration initiatives. Initially, it was hoped that some degree of close cooperation between the newly independent states could be managed through the Commonwealth of Independent States (CIS), created in 1992. However, the CIS largely failed as a vehicle of integration, both because all countries were also absorbed with a deeply painful process of transformation in the 1990s, and also because different clusters of countries began to move closer towards other large, neighbouring economic powers. The central Asian states, for example, shifted towards China and the Middle East, while the Baltic states, Moldova, and Ukraine became much closer to the European Union.

Russia's efforts to forge closer ties with several former Soviet republics culminated in the creation of the Eurasian Customs Union (ECU) in January 2010. Initially this involved Russia, Kazakhstan, and Belarus. The ECU was enlarged in 2015 to include Armenia and Kyrgyzstan, at around the same time that the ECU was transformed into the Eurasian Economic Union (EAEU), a supranational economic bloc that is in many ways modelled along the lines of the European Union. Russian officials, including Vladimir Putin, expressed the hope that the EAEU, with Russia as its driving force, will constitute a strong and dynamic 'pole' in the global economy. Russia's leaders also spoke of the desire to combine the EAEU with China's Belt Road Initiative (BRI) to generate economic growth and development across the Greater Eurasia region.

Russia's state capitalist economy in a globalized world

The system of political economy that was built in Russia over the past three decades is plugged into the wider global economy to a much greater extent than has been the case since Russia emerged as a major global power in the 1500s. It is open to inward flows of trade, capital, and people. Its people own assets across the globe. Russian firms shape the movements of some of the most important sectors in global commerce. And its government seeks to play a part in setting the terms of global economic exchange, both in Eurasia and beyond. All this suggests that Russia is very much a global and outward-looking economic power.

Yet much of Russia's involvement in the global economy, especially in trade, is conducted by entities owned or heavily influenced by the state, reflecting the importance of state control in strategically important sectors of the Russian economy. On occasion, this can lead to friction with other countries that suspect ulterior political motives behind the ostensibly commercial activities of Russian firms. For some observers, the excessive influence of the state is a weakness that prevents Russia from harvesting the full potential of integration with the global economy. But such thinking may prove to be outdated. The blend of outward-looking state capitalism on show in Russia is becoming increasingly common across the world today. Brazil, China, the Gulf States, Saudi Arabia, and Turkey have all shown that state control over key areas of the domestic economy can be successfully combined with an openness to the global economy. If these trends persist, Russia's model of integration may yet prove to be the norm rather than the exception.

Chapter 7
Prospects for the future of the Russian economy

Russia has undergone a number of tumultuous changes over the last hundred years. After the upheaval of the revolution after the defeat in the First World War, rapid industrialization and collectivization changed the fabric of both Russia's economy and that of the other constituent parts of the Soviet Union. The emergence of the Soviet Union as a superpower after the Second World War also imposed an enormous economic cost. Hyper-militarization and the rise of the dependency on oil and gas exports all became deep-rooted characteristics of the Soviet economy, and their influence on the contemporary Russian economy continues to persist. The disintegration of the planned economy and the painful market reforms of the 1990s remain in the memory of many Russians today, helping to explain why the reassertion of state power and authority in the 2000s was welcomed by a large proportion of the population.

The Russian economy today faces a number of different challenges. Some of these are similar to those faced by other countries. Demographic change, for example, is not a uniquely Russian phenomenon, but instead is reshaping all other major economic powers. The same is true of the need to keep up with technological changes and to become competitive in new and emerging industries. And dealing with excessively high and rising regional inequality is a problem faced by many other large, regionally diverse countries. But some of the challenges faced by Russia today are specific to a smaller group of countries. Dealing with changes in global energy production and consumption, for example, will enormously affect all major hydrocarbon producers. Russia's age-old struggle with striking the right balance between state and market is also likely to recur. How policymakers choose to deal with these challenges will determine not only what type of economy prevails for the remainder of the 21st century, but also whether Russia will remain a power of global significance.

Demographic changes

Russia today is in the midst of a profound and complicated demographic transformation. The Russian population fell from nearly 149 million in 1993 to just under 143 million in 2009 (Figure 7). This decline was caused by a sharp dip in birth rates and a corresponding increase in the death rate. Both these trends began in the late 1980s, and caused natural population growth to decline from the early 1990s onwards. Explanations for the rising death rate include a sharp rise in mortality among men below

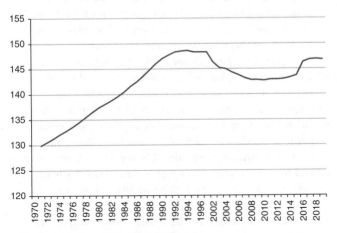

7. **Total population, 1990–2018 (millions).**

50 years old due to alcoholism and other related health problems. The uncertainty and distress caused by the collapse of the Soviet Union in 1991 has been cited as an important factor in causing the decline in the fertility rate. However, this trend was already under way well before the disintegration of the Soviet Union, indicating that the economic pain of the late 1980s and 1990s was an aggravating factor in a wider process.

Population growth resumed in 2011. This was helped by large inflows of immigration from ex-Soviet states, a decline in the death rate, and a modest yet sustained increase in the fertility rate. All three factors were boosted by Russia's strong economic performance since 1999, which created job opportunities for migrant workers, and boosted health and social care provision, which in turn caused an improvement across most health indicators. However, the single most important boost to Russia's population was caused by the illegal annexation of Crimea in 2014, which added around 2.5 million to the total Russian population.

Life expectancy in Russia fell during much of the 1990s. In 1994, life expectancy for men was 57 years and 71 years for women. Such figures had not been seen in Russia since the late 1950s. However, as the death rate began to fall in 2003, life expectancy in Russia began to rise again. Nevertheless, with an average life expectancy of just over 71 years, Russia's population now exhibits a life expectancy comparable with Pakistan, Bangladesh, and Madagascar. The aggregate data also conceal significant regional variation. For instance, life expectancy in Moscow is around 70 years for men and 78 years for women. By contrast, life expectancy in Tuva, on the border of Mongolia, is 55 years for men and 66 years for women. These figures are comparable to life expectancy in low-income sub-Saharan African countries.

Like many of the middle- and high-income countries, Russia's population is ageing rapidly. The improvements in life expectancy made in the 2000s have contributed to the share of people aged 60 or over rising steadily in recent years. Over a fifth of the population is now aged 60 or over (the legal retirement age in Russia was, until 2019, 55 years for women and 60 years for men). As a result of what the economist George Magnus described as the 'age of ageing', the potential labour force in Russia has been shrinking since 2010.

A gradual compression of the demographic space has also taken place across Russia over the past two and a half decades. During the Soviet period, a shift in population towards Russia's eastern regions took place. However, between 1990 and 2015, the population of Russia's Far East Federal District alone fell from 8 million to 6.2 million, a decline of nearly 25 per cent. As the population in the east has declined, the population in the south and central regions has grown. The fastest population growth has occurred in the North Caucasus, where there is a predominantly Muslim population. Within the North Caucasus, the fastest population growth rates have been recorded in Chechnya and Dagestan. This tendency towards faster population growth in Muslim regions is evident within Russia's Federal Districts. For instance, while the overall population of the Volga Federal District shrank over the past decade, six of the seven regions from within the Federal District that registered growth were non-ethnic Russian republics. Population growth in Russia's Central Federal District has been driven primarily by growth in Moscow City where the officially recorded population grew by 12 per cent between 2005 and 2015. This tendency reflected a wider pattern of population growth in larger cities across Russia as people have been attracted to brighter economic prospects.

Demographic prospects and challenges

Russia's official statistical agency, Rosstat, produced a detailed demographic forecast in 2016. The first of these forecasts—the low variant—is based on a simple extrapolation of existing trends.

The second of the forecasts—the medium variant—is based on the assumption that policies undertaken over the past decade and a half will improve health, demographic, and migration outcomes in the years to come. The third forecast—the high variant—is based on the assumption that a comprehensive strategy to deal with demographic change is implemented.

The high variant of the forecast envisages the population growing to over 152 million by 2030, adding nearly 6 million people to the population. By contrast, the low variant sees Russia's population declining to below 143 million by 2030. The difference between the two forecasts is nearly 10 million. The United Nations Population Division's (UNPD) baseline forecast is even more pessimistic about Russia's demographic prospects than the Rosstat low variant. The UNPD envisage that the Russian population will shrink to 138 million by 2030. The divergence between the UNPD and Rosstat forecasts is partially explained by the fact that the UNPD do not include the Crimean population in their calculations. However, the UNPD also base their calculations on more conservative assumptions of Russia's future birth and death rates than those used by Rosstat.

All three Rosstat forecasts are based on the assumption that natural population growth will be negative for most of (in the case of the high variant) or all of the next fifteen years. This will represent a reversal of the modest natural population growth registered in Russia since 2010. In all cases, this tendency will be caused by a gentle yet inexorable rise in the death rate and a modest decline in the birth rate.

Although the natural population growth will, in even the best-case scenario, begin to shrink again over the next five years, the overall size of the population should remain stable as large inflows of migrants from ex-Soviet republics continue to satisfy demand for relatively cheap labour within Russia. Thus, the continuation of robust inward flows of migrants from ex-Soviet republics, especially those of central Asia, is of fundamental importance to Russia's demographic prospects.

The sum of annual inflows of migrants would reach over 3 million people by 2030 in the low variant, and would reach 6.2 million people in the high variant. If we assume that around half of these migrants will come from central Asia, as was the case between 1991 and 2016, then an additional 1.5–3 million migrants from the region will enter Russia over the next decade and a half. Most of these migrants will seek work in Russia's largest cities where economic prospects are brightest and demand for low-wage labour is strongest.

Due to improvements in public health provision, as well as changes in the lifestyle of Russians born after the collapse of the Soviet Union, life expectancy at birth is expected to rise in all three forecasts. In the low variant, overall life expectancy is forecast to reach 73.2 in 2030. This is comparable with life expectancy in El Salvador and Libya in 2018. Even under the high variant, life expectancy at birth is only expected to reach 77.3 by 2030. This is comparable with life expectancy in Poland and Bosnia and Herzegovina in 2018.

The large gap between male and female life expectancy will continue to persist, regardless of the forecast. This is likely to result in a permanent gender imbalance in the over-60 age group, although the gender gap will not affect younger age groups to the same extent.

The dependency ratio—that is, the number of the non-working population supported by the population of working age—should rise sharply until the mid-2020s. The labour force is projected to decline in absolute terms in the lower (reduction of 6 million people) and medium (reduction of 4 million people) variants, although the high variant forecasts a modest upturn in the size of the labour force from the early 2020s onwards, leading to total reduction of the labour force of around 2 million people by 2030.

As the labour force continues to shrink—both in absolute terms and as a share of the population—demand for migrant labour should continue to grow in Russia's largest cities, where demand for unskilled labour to work in the service sector is likely to be highest. As a result of this contraction in the labour force and rise in number of pensioners, government spending on pensions will continue to rise, causing a reduction in resources available to meet other social and political objectives.

Population growth will be faster in the large cities and in southern, Muslim parts of the country. This will lead to a gradual shift in the ethnic composition of Russia as a whole, although it is unlikely to manifest itself in Russia's largely Slavic regions in the north and west of the country. By contrast, population growth in Russia's northern and far eastern regions will continue to decline as federal resources prove insufficient to subsidize large numbers of dependent groups.

These changes, which are forecast to take place over the next few decades, will present policymakers with serious challenges. Some remote areas, such as the Arctic and the Far East, are likely to suffer from continued depopulation. This tendency has already affected rural areas, as well. In contrast, big cities are beginning to suffer from overpopulation. Rising populations in cities demand investment in supporting infrastructure, but this has yet to take place. Rising immigration may also cause social tensions to rise. An ageing population is also likely to impose rapidly growing demands on Russia's welfare and health systems. Additional financial resources will be needed, but finding these may prove difficult given the other important areas of public spending that currently absorb government resources, such as defence.

Regional variation

Russia is the largest country in the world. This means that any data that refer to average levels (income, economic structure, life expectancy, etc.) at the national level conceal huge variations across Russia's eighty-four regions. Some of these regions, like Krasnoyarsk Krai, are geographically larger than western Europe. Research from the Independent Institute of Social Policy (IISP) in Moscow has shown that the Russian population can be differentiated according to four broad categories.

The 'first' Russia consists of residents of Russia's major cities (i.e. those with populations of over a half a million, accounting for around 30 per cent of Russia's total population). The proportion of Russians living in these large cities grew due to an influx of migrants attracted to the economic opportunities offered. Such cities tend to be characterized by post-industrial economic structures (i.e. a high share of services in the local economy), high per capita income, and a large share of middle-class citizens (30–40 per cent of the population). For residents of 'first' Russia, integration with and exposure to the global economy is relatively high. People have access to a wide range of goods and services, travel frequently, and have access to the Internet. Crime rates also tend to be much lower, and the average age tends to be lower.

A 'second' Russia is said to reside in cities with populations of between 50,000 and 500,000 people (around 40 per cent of the population). Human and financial resources are insufficient to support wider socio-economic and political modernization. The economic structure of such cities tends to be dominated either by archaic Soviet-era industrial activities, or by public sector employment. In Russia's provincial towns and cities, incomes tend to be lower, the average age higher, and people have access to a more restricted range of goods and services. Such cities tend to be less well integrated with the global economy, and have experienced an outflow of the younger segment of their populations, who have often emigrated to 'first' Russia or abroad in search of greater opportunities. Health and educational outcomes in these parts of Russia are considerably poorer than in 'first' Russia.

The IISP further identify a 'third' and 'fourth' Russia, which encompasses the rural areas of Russia, as well as the residents of villages and small towns with a population of less than 20,000 (collectively accounting for around a third of the population).

In these cities, educational and health provision and outcomes are poor, and social mobility is low. The public sector and agriculture provide most formal employment and many people work in the informal sector. These rural regions are increasingly characterized by shrinking populations, gender imbalances among the older segments of the population, low or reduced investment in public services and social infrastructure, and low skill levels.

The disparities in regional economic development described by the IISP are, to a significant degree, caused by the sheer size of Russia. Roughly three-quarters of Russia's 146 million population resides west of the Ural Mountains in what can be broadly described as 'European Russia'. European Russia, however, only accounts for around a quarter of Russia's territory. The remaining quarter of the population are dispersed across the vast territory located east of the Urals where the distances to and between other population centres are long. The climate is also inhospitable for large parts of the year. This combination of long distances and inhospitable climatic conditions raises transport and production costs, and impedes economic development. A World Bank report, published in 2011, highlighted the important role that reducing 'spatial inefficiency' will play in boosting Russia's economic competitiveness in the future.

Meeting the challenge of dealing with vast regional inequality will certainly require significant financial resources. After all, boosting investment in deprived areas, or building new infrastructure to increase connectivity between urban hubs across the huge country, is expensive. The main question is whether the federal state (i.e. Moscow) takes responsibility for this, or whether it is delegated to either regional state authorities or the market.

The need for investment and innovation

Future economic growth must also be investment based if Russia is to diversify and modernize its economic base. However, the level of investment in new factories, machinery, and infrastructure in Russia has been and remains low, relative to other middle-income countries. Investment as a proportion of GDP declined over the 1990s, reaching a post-socialist low of 14 per cent in 1999, before rebounding to a post-socialist high of 22 per cent in 2008. It has remained at around the 20 per cent level since. This is problematic because low- and middle-income economies engaged in the 'catch-up' process are typically expected to register investment rates of 25–35 per cent.

Partially as a result of this low rate of investment, the size of high-technology and knowledge-intensive sectors remains relatively small, and where they do exist, they are dominated by state and military organizations, such as in arms production and nuclear power generation machinery. There are some promising areas where the private sector is dominant, such as software, but these are modest in size compared to Russia's other leading sectors in the natural resources sector.

Again, the biggest question in the realm of industrial and technology policy is whether the state will retain the leading role that it has historically occupied, especially in sectors it considers to be of strategic importance. Russia has many of the ingredients required for innovation, not least a population that is highly educated by global standards. Unfortunately, it also suffers from a very poor incentive structure for innovation: weak property rights, low levels of competition, and an often-overbearing state remain serious obstacles. Without dealing with these problems, responsibility for technological development will primarily lie with the state.

A weak financial sector

The poor standard of financial intermediation in Russia is also a chronic problem. The domestic financial sector emerged from being virtually non-existent for most of the Soviet period—with private banks only appearing in the late 1980s—to become an important part of the contemporary Russian economy. It is, however, small compared with the financial sectors of other countries. The total volume of credit extended to the private sector amounted to just over 55 per cent of GDP. By contrast, this figure is close to or in excess of 100 per cent in many other middle-income countries. Russia's financial system is also overwhelmingly bankcentric with very limited alternative sources of finance available to prospective borrowers. Perhaps most importantly, the financial sector is dominated by state-owned or state-controlled banks. Around two-thirds of financial assets are held by banks owned by, or with close links to, the state. These banks provide capital to larger enterprises, also with close links to the state, at either the federal or regional level. However, the market for long-term capital is extremely shallow, leaving most enterprises to rely on their own resources (such as retained earnings) to generate capital for investment.

The weakness of the financial system ensures that politically influential enterprises—especially in Sector B where enterprises have close links to the state—have access to capital, but also that many SMEs and entrepreneurs are cut off from access to capital.

Sector A firms—globally competitive energy and mining companies—have been able to access international capital markets and therefore have been relatively unaffected by the weakness of the domestic financial sector. Breaking the stranglehold that large, politically well-connected firms have over access to capital will help deal with many of the other problems facing the Russian economy. For example, if smaller firms are able to access capital—and are confident that they will keep any return on their investment—then it is possible that private investment might accelerate. This should in turn boost the prospects for diversification and technological development.

The problem of energy dependence

Because oil and gas exports play such a critical role in shaping the economic prospects of the country, any changes in the global energy market are likely to significantly affect Russia. In recent years, two important developments emerged which have the potential to revolutionize the way in which the international oil market functions: the so-called 'shale revolution' in the United States, which has seen it become the world's largest oil producer; and the sharp reduction in the price of renewable power generation, primarily in the form of solar power and wind turbines. The shale revolution has led many to suggest that oil is no longer a scarce commodity, but instead is now abundant. As a result, the supply of oil on global markets is no longer seen as under threat. At the same time, the rapid growth of renewable power generation is threatening to reduce the role played by hydrocarbons—especially coal and gas—in power generation. The urgent need to meet global climate change objectives contained in the Paris Agreement makes the expansion of renewables all the more imperative. The apparent abundance of oil, on the hand, and the need to constrain demand for oil, on the other, have the potential to suppress oil prices permanently and, in doing so, reduce the value of Russia's primary source of export revenue.

Together, these trends present an especially serious challenge to Russia for two reasons. First, although official policy rhetoric in recent years emphasized the importance of developing non-energy industries, in practice the role of hydrocarbons grew. In all but one year between 2010 and 2018, investment in the hydrocarbons sectors grew faster than the overall rate of investment in the wider economy. This means that the role of oil and gas in the Russian economy is growing rather than diminishing. Second, official efforts to foster the emergence of manufacturing and, apparently, diversify the country's economic structure are in fact dependent on the existence of a thriving oil and gas industry. Twelve of the nineteen non-military areas of the economy identified by the government's import substitution strategy of 2015 were in the oil and gas extraction equipment industry. Elsewhere, grand state-directed plans to develop the shipbuilding industry in Russia's Far East were based on projected demand from Russian energy companies for ships and marine equipment to facilitate offshore oil and gas extraction.

It is clear that current economic policy in Russia is based on optimistic projections for future energy sales, and appears designed to prolong rather than ease the dependence of the wider Russian economy on hydrocarbons. If changes in the global energy order result in lower prices for Russia's oil and gas exports, it is possible that Russia's economy will suffer yet again from its overdependence on energy sales.

Reducing the defence burden

There are different ways to measure the extent of military expenditure in a country. One of the most widely used is produced annually by the Stockholm International Peace Research Institute (SIPRI). According to SIPRI, Russian military expenditure has fluctuated between roughly 4 and 5 per cent of GDP over the past decade. This is significantly higher than the same measure for Russia's European neighbours to the west, who struggle to spend

2 per cent of GDP on the military, and its Asian neighbours to the south and east. While the extent of the defence burden is nowhere near as extreme as during the Soviet period, it is also true that the comparatively high share of defence in government spending means fewer resources are available for other areas of public spending that are starved of resources. Moreover, defence expenditure is dominated by state-owned enterprises. Such firms are dependent on government spending and have only limited incentives to promote greater efficiency.

Reducing the defence burden to a level comparable with the global average is, however, something that few Russian rulers have ever succeeded in doing. This is because the need for a strong and independent military to deal with a wide range of threats—both internal and external—is firmly rooted in both history and geography. Shifting spending away from defence and security will prove even more difficult at the current time due to the elevated tensions between Russia, on the one hand, and the United States and its allies, on the other. Unfortunately, for as long as Russia's sense of insecurity remains high it is likely that scarce resources will continue to be diverted to relatively unproductive defence expenditure.

Strengthening the market?

According to many critical observers, the Putinist system of political economy is no longer capable of generating the rates of investment and growth needed for Russia to prosper and to respond to the myriad challenges facing it. As evidence, they point to the fact that GDP in 2018 was barely higher than it was in 2013. Investment has also struggled to pick up over the same period. Proposals for reform have come from many directions, including from within the ruling elite and from outside experts in the International Monetary Fund (IMF) and European Bank for Reconstruction and Development (EBRD). Many of the proposals put forward by these sources are held in common and can be said to constitute a 'liberal' critique of the excessive role played by the state in the current system of political economy.

According to these proposals, the revenues generated by Sector A should be managed more efficiently. In order to ensure that hydrocarbon production does not drop, and with it the main source of government tax revenues, it has been suggested that reform of the regulatory and legal frameworks for the energy industry is urgently required, which in turn might incentivize innovation and efficiency. Most critics of the current system also recommend reducing the support given to Sector B. This could be achieved by continuing with politically unpopular pension and welfare reforms, reducing military spending and the support given to inefficient industrial enterprises, and formulating industrial policies that do not perpetuate the country's dependence on hydrocarbon sales. Collectively, these measures have the potential to reduce both the state's role in economic management and the number of people that rely on its support.

Of equal importance is the urgent need to promote investment and economic activity in Sector C. If these measures were to be successful, new and efficient firms might emerge to replace older, more inefficient firms. This could ease the pressure on the federal budget, enhance competition across the economy, and ultimately promote the goal of modernization and diversification. Such transformation would emerge 'from below', or through the market, rather than through the state-led measures traditionally employed by Russia's rulers. The most widely proposed reform is aimed at strengthening property rights and the legal system more broadly, and, by doing so, raising the incentive for businesses to invest.

These proposals are relatively uncontroversial. They are, however, dependent on some form of political reform. Strengthening the rule of law, for example, would constrain the ability of powerful individuals to use public office for personal gain. This would make it more difficult for Russia's political rulers to redistribute economic resources to garner political support. Moreover, painful reforms that would generate greater unemployment and economic dislocation have proven difficult to implement. The memory of the 1990s is important in this respect. For as long as large swathes of the population view the state as a source of stability and the market as a source of pain there will be clear limits to what type of reform is feasible.

There are also externally imposed limits to the types of reform that are possible. When Russia has faced growing external threats—whether real or perceived—powerful groups within the ruling elite have used security concerns to justify measures to create a stronger and more activist state. This is precisely what happened in the aftermath of Russia's confrontation with the West following the outbreak of conflict in Ukraine in 2014. Revenues from Sector A continued to drive economic activity. At the same time, the growth of military expenditure after 2013, along with the increase in support directed at 'strategic' areas of the economy, boosted Sector B. Sector C continued to suffer from poor property rights and a business climate that favours the politically well connected. Put simply, economic policy since 2014 served to reinforce the Putinist system of political economy rather than change it.

Taken together, these internal and external obstacles to reform appear insurmountable in the absence of any sudden and unexpected changes, at least in the short term. Looking to the future, the Russian analyst Dmitry Trenin argued that 'Russia's political economy will have a corporate socio-political structure, with the Kremlin continuing to play the role of an arbiter among the principal vested interests'. This suggests that the Putinist model of political economy might well live on even after its architect has disappeared from the political scene. Indeed, given the repeated resistance of those in the state to the expansion of the market throughout Russian history, predicting anything other than continued state dominance, at least of the 'commanding heights' of the economy, would seem excessively optimistic. What is perhaps more feasible is for Russia's leaders to make a more concerted effort at disciplining the state and encouraging it to become more efficient and perhaps even humane. Promoting the rule of law within Russia's elite would be the best place to start if Russia is to make serious progress in its centuries-long quest to 'tame the state'.

References

Chapter 1: Forces that shaped the economy in Russia

Vladimir Putin, 'Rossiia na rubezhe tysiacheletii' [Russia at the turn of the millennium], *Nezavisimaia Gazeta*, 30 December 1999. English translation available in: Vladimir Putin, *First Person* (Public Affairs Group, 2000)

Robert Gilpin, *Global Political Economy* (Princeton University Press, 2004), pp. 148–9

Geoffrey Hosking, *Russian History: A Very Short Introduction* (Oxford University Press, 2012), p. 19

Yegor Gaidar, *Russia: The Long View* (MIT Press, 2012), p. 312

Gaidar, *Russia*, p. 332

Steven Rosefielde and Stefan Hedlund, *Russia Since 1980* (Cambridge University Press, 2009), p. 12

Chapter 2: The Soviet planned economy

Vladimir Kontorovich, *Reluctant Cold Warriors* (Oxford University Press, 2019), p. 3

Janos Kornai, *The Socialist System* (Cambridge University Press, 1992)

Yegor Gaidar, *Collapse of an Empire* (Brookings Institution Press, 2006), pp. 205–10

Chapter 3: The creation of a market

Yegor Gaidar, *Russia: The Long View* (MIT Press, 2012), p. 347

Chapter 4: The reassertion of the state

Vladimir Putin, 'Rossiia na rubezhe tysiacheletii' [Russia at the turn
    of the millennium], *Nezavisimaia Gazeta*, 30 December 1999.
    English translation available in: Vladimir Putin, *First Person*
    (Public Affairs Group, 2000)

Chapter 5: From modernization to isolation

Dmitry Medvedev, 'Go Russia!' 10 September 2009. Available at:
    <http://en.kremlin.ru/events/president/news/5413>
Vladimir Putin, 'Nam nuzhna novaya ekonomika' [We need a new
    economy], *Vedomosti*, 30 January 2012. Available at: <https://
    www.vedomosti.ru/politics/articles/2012/01/30/o_nashih_
    ekonomicheskih_zadachah>
Clifford Gaddy and Barry Ickes, *Can Sanctions Stop Putin's Russia?*
    3 June 2014, available at: <https://www.brookings.edu/articles/
    can-sanctions-stop-putin/>

Chapter 7: Prospects for the future of the Russian economy

World Bank, *Russia: Reshaping Economic Geography* (World Bank,
    2011), available at: <http://documents.worldbank.org/curated/
    en/863281468107678371/pdf/629050ESW0box30g0Economic0G
    eography.pdf>
SIPRI, *Military Expenditure Database* (SIPRI), available at:
    <https://www.sipri.org/databases/milex>
Dmitry Trenin, *Russia* (Polity, 2019), p. 179

Further reading

Chapter 1: Forces that shaped the economy in Russia

Yegor Gaidar, *Russia: The Long View* (MIT Press, 2012)

Stefan Hedlund, *Russian Path Dependence* (Routledge, 2005)

Geoffrey Hosking, *Russia and the Russians* (Penguin, 2001)

Richard Pipes, *Russia Under the Old Regime* (Penguin, 1974)

Vladimir Shlapentokh and Anna Arutunyan, *Freedom, Repression, and Private Property in Russia* (Cambridge University Press, 2013)

Andrei Tsygankov, *The Strong State in Russia: Development and Crisis* (Oxford University Press, 2015)

Chapter 2: The Soviet planned economy

R. W. Davies, *Soviet Economic Development from Lenin to Khrushchev* (Cambridge University Press, 1998)

Yegor Gaidar, *Collapse of an Empire* (Brookings Institution Press, 2006)

Philip Hanson, *The Rise and Fall of the Soviet Economy* (Pearson Press, 2002)

Vladimir Kontorovich, *Reluctant Cold Warriors* (Oxford University Press, 2019)

Janos Kornai, *The Socialist System* (Cambridge University Press, 1992)

Silvana Malle, *The Economic Organisation of War Communism, 1918–21* (Cambridge University Press, 1983)

Alec Nove, *The Economic History of the USSR* (Penguin, 1982)

Chapter 3: The creation of a market

Peter Aven and Alfred Kokh, *Gaidar's Revolution: The Inside Account of the Economic Transformation of Russia* (I. B. Tauris, 2013)

Chrystia Freeland, *Sale of the Century: Russia's Wild Ride from Communism to Capitalism* (Crown Business, 1999)

Clifford Gaddy and Barry Ickes, *Russia's Virtual Economy* (Brookings Institution Press, 2002)

David Hoffman, *The Oligarchs: Wealth, and Power in the New Russia* (Public Affairs, 2002)

Stephen Kotkin, *Armageddon Averted: The Soviet Collapse 1970–2000* (Oxford University Press, 2001)

Andrei Shleifer and Daniel Treisman, *Without a Map: Political Tactics and Economic Reform in Russia* (MIT Press, 2000)

Chapter 4: The reassertion of the state

Stephen Fortescue, *Russia's Oil Barons and Metal Magnates: Oligarchs and the State in Transition* (Palgrave Macmillan, 2006)

Thane Gustafson, *The Wheel of Fortune: The Battle for Oil and Power in Russia* (Harvard University Press, 2012)

Alena Ledeneva, *Can Russia Modernise?* (Cambridge University Press, 2012)

Vladimir Putin, *First Person: An Astonishingly Frank Self-Portrait by Russia's President* (Public Affairs, 2000)

Richard Sakwa, *Putin and the Oligarch* (I. B. Tauris, 2014)

Pekka Sutela, *The Political Economy of Putin's Russia* (Routledge, 2012)

Chapter 5: From modernization to isolation

Richard Connolly, *Russia's Response to Sanctions* (Cambridge University Press, 2018)

Vladimir Mau, *Russia's Economy in an Epoch of Turbulence* (Routledge, 2018)

Chris Miller, *Putinomics: Power and Money in Resurgent Russia* (University of North Carolina Press, 2016)

Steven Rosefielde and Stefan Hedlund, *Russia Since 1980: Wrestling with Westernisation* (Cambridge University Press, 2009)

Daniel Treisman, *The Return: Russia's Journey from Gorbachev to Medvedev* (Free Press, 2011)

Grigory Yavlinsky, *The Putin System: An Opposing View* (Columbia University Press, 2019)

Chapter 6: Russia in the global economy

Glenn Diesen, *Russia's Geoeconomic Strategy for the Greater Eurasia* (Routledge, 2017)

Stefan Hedlund, *Putin's Energy Agenda: The Contradictions of Russia's Resource Wealth* (Lynne Rienner, 2014)

Sergei Kulik, Nikita Maslennikov, and Igor Yurgens, *At a Crossroads: Russia in the Global Economy* (Centre for International Governance Innovation, 2019)

Bobo Lo, *A Wary Embrace: What the China-Russia Relationship Means for the World* (Penguin, 2017)

Alexander Lukin, *Russia and China: The New Rapprochement* (Polity, 2018)

Chapter 7: Prospects for the future of the Russian economy

Timothy Frye, *Property Rights and Property Wrongs* (Cambridge University Press, 2018)

Clifford Gaddy and Barry Ickes, *Bear Traps on Russia's Road to Modernisation* (Routledge, 2013)

Loren Graham, *Lonely Ideas* (MIT Press, 2014)

Kathryn Hendley, *Everyday Law in Russia* (Cornell University Press, 2017)

Richard Sakwa, *Russia's Futures* (Polity, 2019)

Index

For the benefit of digital users, indexed terms that span two pages (e.g., 52–53) may, on occasion, appear on only one of those pages.

INNOVATION
A Very Short Introduction
Mark Dodgson & David Gann

This *Very Short Introduction* looks at what innovation is and why it affects us so profoundly. It examines how it occurs, who stimulates it, how it is pursued, and what its outcomes are, both positive and negative. Innovation is hugely challenging and failure is common, yet it is essential to our social and economic progress. Mark Dodgson and David Gann consider the extent to which our understanding of innovation developed over the past century and how it might be used to interpret the global economy we all face in the future.

'Innovation has always been fundamental to leadership, be it in the public or private arena. This insightful book teaches lessons from the successes of the past, and spotlights the challenges and the opportunities for innovation as we move from the industrial age to the knowledge economy.'

Sanford, Senior Vice President, IBM

www.oup.com/vsi

Modern China
A Very Short Introduction
Rana Mitter

China today is never out of the news: from human rights
controversies and the continued legacy of Tiananmen Square,
to global coverage of the Beijing Olympics, and the Chinese
'economic miracle'. It seems a country of contradictions: a
peasant society with some of the world's most futuristic cities,
heir to an ancient civilization that is still trying to find a modern
identity. This *Very Short Introduction* offers the reader with no
previous knowledge of China a variety of ways to understand
the world's most populous nation, giving a short, integrated
picture of modern Chinese society, culture, economy, politics
and art.

'A brilliant essay.'

Timothy Garton, TLS

THE FIRST WORLD WAR

A Very Short Introduction

Michael Howard

By the time the First World War ended in 1918, eight million people had died in what had been perhaps the most apocalyptic episode the world had known. This *Very Short Introduction* provides a concise and insightful history of the 'Great War', focusing on why it happened, how it was fought, and why it had the consequences it did. It examines the state of Europe in 1914 and the outbreak of war; the onset of attrition and crisis; the role of the US; the collapse of Russia; and the weakening and eventual surrender of the Central Powers. Looking at the historical controversies surrounding the causes and conduct of war, Michael Howard also describes how peace was ultimately made, and the potent legacy of resentment left to Germany.

'succinct, comprehensive and beautifully written. Indeed reading it is an experience comparable to scanning the clues of a well-composed crossword puzzle. Every allusion is eventually supplied with an answer, and the finished product defies the puzzler's disbelief that the intricacies can be brought to a convincing conclusion.... Michael Howard is the master of the short book'

TLS

MODERN JAPAN
A Very Short Introduction
Christopher Goto-Jones

Japan is arguably today's most successful industrial economy, combining almost unprecedented affluence with social stability and apparent harmony. Japanese goods and cultural products are consumed all over the world, ranging from animated movies and computer games all the way through to cars, semiconductors, and management techniques. In many ways, Japan is an icon of the modern world, and yet it remains something of an enigma to many, who see it as a confusing montage of the alien and the familiar, the ancient and modern. The aim of this Very Short Introduction is to explode the myths and explore the reality of modern Japan - by taking a concise look at its history, economy, politics, and culture.

'A wonderfully engaging narrative of a complicated history, which from the beginning to end sheds light on the meaning of modernity in Japan as it changed over time. An exemplary text.'

Carol Gluck, Columbia University

GEOPOLITICS
A Very Short Introduction
Klaus Dodds

In certain places such as Iraq or Lebanon, moving a few feet either side of a territorial boundary can be a matter of life or death, dramatically highlighting the connections between place and politics. For a country's location and size as well as its sovereignty and resources all affect how the people that live there understand and interact with the wider world. Using wide-ranging examples, from historical maps to James Bond films and the rhetoric of political leaders like Churchill and George W. Bush, this Very Short Introduction shows why, for a full understanding of contemporary global politics, it is not just smart - it is essential - to be geopolitical.

'Engrossing study of a complex topic.'

Mick Herron, Geographical.